GO EXPLORE

NATIONAL PARKS

IF FOUND, PLEASE RETURN TO:

....

....

WILD simplicity
Paper Co. x Est. 2019

Copyright © 2019-2021 by Wild Simplicity Paper Co.

Wild Simplicity Paper Co. supports copyright. Copyright fuels creativity, encourages diverse voices, promotes free speech, and creates a vibrant culture. Thank you for buying an authorized edition of this book and for complying with copyright laws by not reproducing, scanning, or distributing any part of it in any form without permission. You are supporting writers and allowing Wild Simplicity Paper Co. to continue to independently publish thoughtfully designed notebooks, planners, and journals.

For wholesale information or to request a custom book design, write: hello@wildsimplicitypaper.com

ISBN: 9798786987028

Third Edition: December 2021

Printed in the United States

Book Design by Wild Simplicity Paper Co.
wildsimplicitypaper.com

WANT A FREE NATIONAL PARKS GIFT?

Write an honest review of this national parks journal on Amazon and send a screenshot of your posted review to **hello@wildsimplicitypaper.com**. We'll reply with some national parks-related gifts you can print at home to plan and remember your adventures! (Bonus points — and extra goodies! — if you include photos in your review.)

MAP OF THE 63 U.S. NATIONAL PARKS

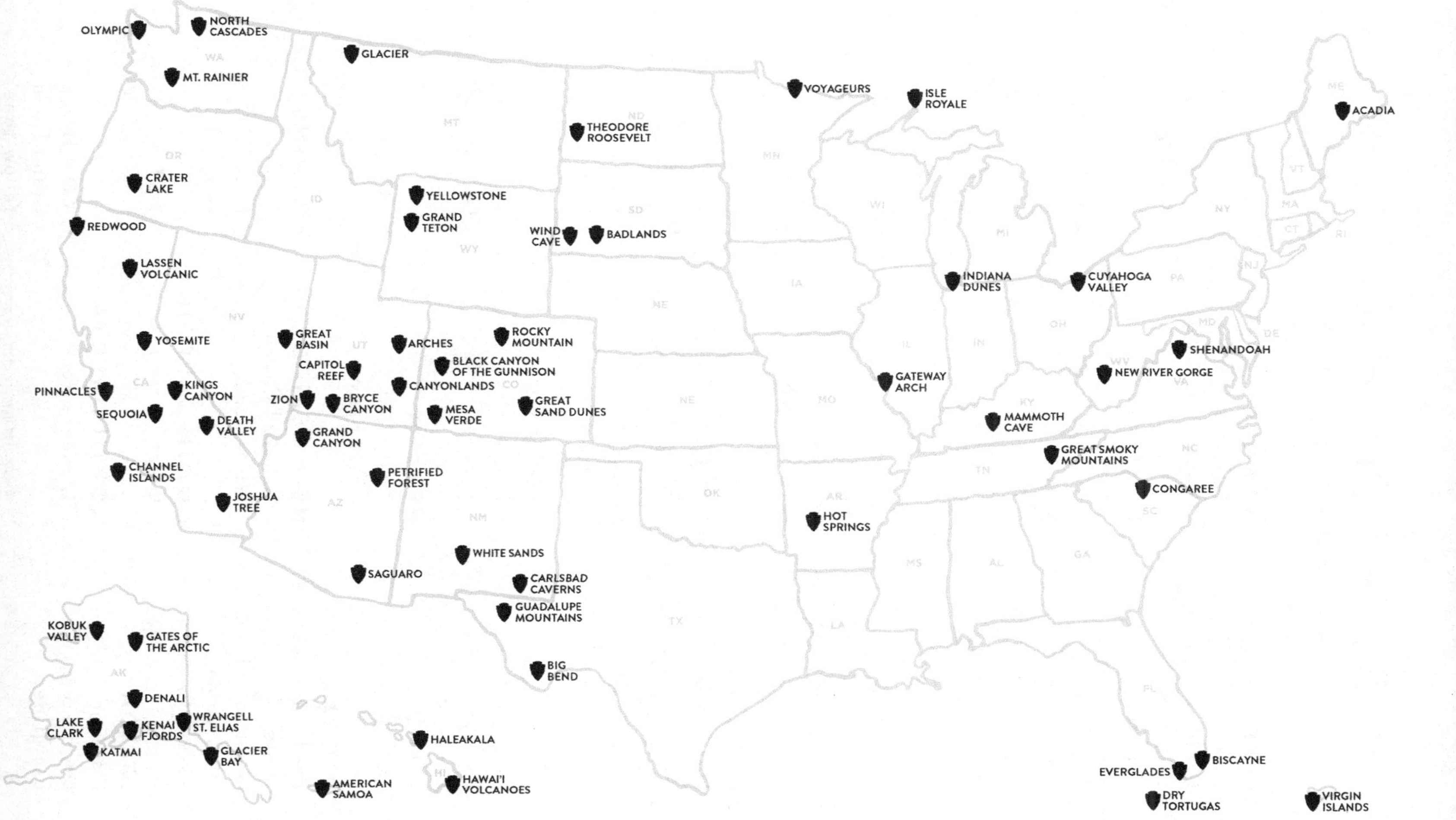

U.S. NATIONAL PARKS
BUCKET LIST BY STATE

ALASKA
Denali
Gates of the Arctic
Glacier Bay
Katmai
Kenai Fjords
Kobuk Valley
Lake Clark
Wrangell-St. Elias

AMERICAN SAMOA
American Samoa

ARIZONA
Grand Canyon
Petrified Forest
Saguaro

ARKANSAS
Hot Springs

CALIFORNIA
Channel Islands
Death Valley*
Joshua Tree
Kings Canyon
Lassen Volcanic
Pinnacles
Redwood
Sequoia
Yosemite

COLORADO
Black Canyon of the Gunnison
Great Sand Dunes
Mesa Verde
Rocky Mountain

FLORIDA
Biscayne
Dry Tortugas
Everglades

HAWAI'I
Haleakala
Hawai'i Volcanoes

KENTUCKY
Mammoth Cave

IDAHO
Yellowstone*

INDIANA
Indiana Dunes

MAINE
Acadia

MICHIGAN
Isle Royale

MINNESOTA
Voyageurs

MISSOURI
Gateway Arch

MONTANA
Glacier
Yellowstone*

NEVADA
Death Valley*
Great Basin

NEW MEXICO
Carlsbad Caverns
White Sands

NORTH CAROLINA
Great Smoky Mtns*

NORTH DAKOTA
Theodore Roosevelt

*= park located in more than one state

OHIO
Cuyahoga Valley

OREGON
Crater Lake

SOUTH CAROLINA
Congaree

SOUTH DAKOTA
Badlands
Wind Cave

TENNESSEE
Great Smoky Mtns*

TEXAS
Big Bend
Guadalupe Mountains

UTAH
Arches
Bryce Canyon
Canyonlands
Capitol Reef
Zion

VIRGIN ISLANDS
Virgin Islands

VIRGINIA
Shenandoah

WASHINGTON
Mount Rainier
North Cascades
Olympic

WEST VIRGINIA
New River Gorge

WYOMING
Grand Teton
Yellowstone*

COMMON NATIONAL PARK SIGNS & ICONS

- Campground
- Drinking Water
- Ranger Station
- Trailhead
- Wildlife Viewing
- Observation Area
- Showers
- Wheelchair Accessible
- Lodging
- RV Campground
- Four-Wheel-Drive Road
- Swimming Allowed
- Picnic Area

MY NP PACKING LIST:

- [ ]
- [ ]
- [ ]
- [ ]
- [ ]
- [ ]
- [ ]
- [ ]
- [ ]
- [ ]
- [ ]
- [ ]
- [ ]
- [ ]
- [ ]
- [ ]
- [ ]
- [ ]
- [ ]
- [ ]
- [ ]
- [ ]
- [ ]
- [ ]
- [ ]
- [ ]
- [ ]
- [ ]
- [ ]

HOW TO USE THIS JOURNAL

Welcome to our bestselling, newly updated national parks journal featuring all 63 of the U.S. National Parks! We hope this adventure guide and passport stamps log becomes a cherished memory-keeper for you as you venture from park to park.

Franchesca Winters
CEO, Wild Simplicity Paper Co.

DATES, WEATHER & WILDLIFE
Record the date(s) of your trip and the weather you experienced as well as the wildlife you viewed.

TRAVELING COMPANIONS
List the people who accompanied you on your national park visit.

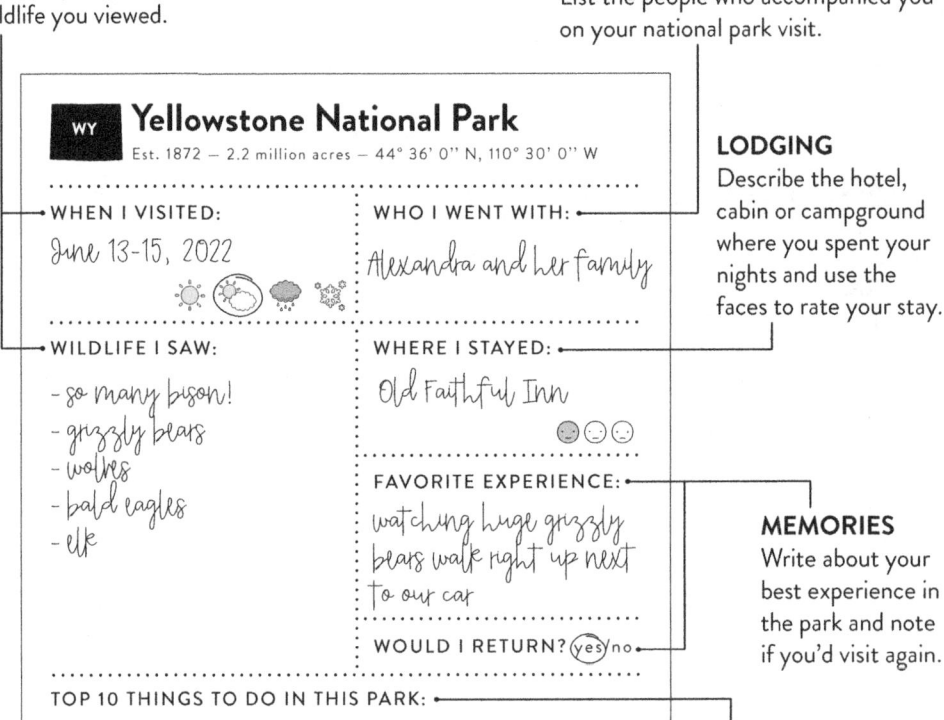

Yellowstone National Park
WY — Est. 1872 — 2.2 million acres — 44° 36' 0" N, 110° 30' 0" W

WHEN I VISITED:
June 13-15, 2022

WHO I WENT WITH:
Alexandra and her family

WILDLIFE I SAW:
- so many bison!
- grizzly bears
- wolves
- bald eagles
- elk

WHERE I STAYED:
Old Faithful Inn

FAVORITE EXPERIENCE:
watching huge grizzly bears walk right up next to our car

WOULD I RETURN? (yes)/no

LODGING
Describe the hotel, cabin or campground where you spent your nights and use the faces to rate your stay.

TOP 10 THINGS TO DO IN THIS PARK:
- ★★★☆☆ Witness the famous eruption of Old Faithful
- ★★★☆☆ Peer into Morning Glory Pool in Upper Geyser Basin
- ★★★☆☆ Take a stroll on the boardwalk along the Grand Prismatic Spring
- ☆☆☆☆☆ Hike through the lodgepole forest to Fairy Falls
- ★★★★★ See the Grand Canyon of the Yellowstone from the South Rim
- ★★★★★ Observe the park's iconic bison herds in Lamar Valley
- ★★★☆☆ Drive or bike the 19-mile Dunraven Pass
- ☆☆☆☆☆ Enjoy panoramic views from the peak of Mt. Washburn
- ★★★☆☆ Visit the travertine terraces of Mammoth Hot Springs
- ★★☆☆☆ Swim in the Boiling River Hot Springs in Gardner River

MEMORIES
Write about your best experience in the park and note if you'd visit again.

TOP 10 ACTIVITIES
From traversing glaciers to sledding down sand dunes, we've included the Top 10 things to do in each park. Use our list of recommendations to plan the trip of a lifetime!

RATE YOUR EXPERIENCES
Fill in the stars to remember what you loved and what you didn't.

MY PARK RATINGS:

- ACTIVITIES: FEW — MANY
- SCENERY: DULL — SPECTACULAR
- PEOPLE: CROWDED — PEACEFUL
- WILDLIFE: NONE — LOTS
- OVERALL: NOT FOR ME — LOVED IT!

MOST MEMORABLE MOMENTS:

Walking the boardwalk through the Grand Prismatic Spring and driving through Lamar Valley were my favorite parts of our visit. I don't remember exactly where we were when we saw the grizzlies but that was by far the best part of the trip.

SPACE TO JOURNAL / DRAW / COLLECT OFFICIAL NATIONAL PARK PASSPORT STAMPS:

Yellowstone National Park — Old Faithful Visitor Center — JUN 13 2022

RATE EACH PARK
Color in the bars to rate the activities, scenery, crowds, wildlife and overall experience of your national park visit.

JOURNAL
What made your visit memorable? Standing beneath one of the world's tallest trees? Kayaking alongside whales in Alaska's glacial waters? Write it down and never forget the moments that took your breath away.

FREE SPACE
How you use this space is entirely up to you!

CREATE-YOUR-OWN BUCKET LISTS
The back of your journal contains five blank bucket lists. What do you want to experience in the national parks?

GET CREATIVE
Choose a theme and list 10 items you want to include in your bucket list. Maybe they're all in one park, maybe they're in 10 different parks. It's up to you!

COMPLETION DATE
Once you've completed your bucket list, add the date!

BUCKET LIST: My Top 10 California NP Hiking Trails

1. Redwood Creek Trail (16 miles)
   Date: January 4, 2022
   National Park: Redwood

2. Ryan Mountain Trail (3 miles)
   Date:
   National Park: Joshua Tree

3. High Peaks Loop (5 miles)
   Date: March 20, 2022
   National Park: Pinnacles

4. Pohono Trail (12 miles)
   Date:
   National Park: Yosemite

5. Brokeoff Mountain Trail (7.6 miles)
   Date:
   National Park: Lassen Volcanic

6. Trail of the Sequoias (7.5 miles)
   Date: August 10, 2022
   National Park: Sequoia

7. Paradise Valley Trail (18.2 miles)
   Date: August 12, 2022
   National Park: Kings Canyon

8. Half Dome Trail (14 miles)
   Date:
   National Park: Yosemite

9. Alta Peak Trail (14.9 miles)
   Date: August 11, 2022
   National Park: Sequoia

10. Potato Harbor Overlook Trail (5 miles)
    Date:
    National Park: Channel Islands

COMPLETED ON:

Acadia National Park

Est. 1919 — 48,996 acres — 44° 20' 20" N, 68° 16' 24" W

WHEN I VISITED:

WHO I WENT WITH:

WILDLIFE I SAW:

WHERE I STAYED:

FAVORITE EXPERIENCE:

WOULD I RETURN? yes/no

TOP 10 THINGS TO DO IN THIS PARK:

☆ ☆ ☆ ☆ ☆ Watch the sunrise from the top of Cadillac Mountain
☆ ☆ ☆ ☆ ☆ Dip your toes in the ocean at Sand Beach
☆ ☆ ☆ ☆ ☆ Listen to the waves crash at Thunder Hole
☆ ☆ ☆ ☆ ☆ Drive or bike the 27-mile Park Loop Road
☆ ☆ ☆ ☆ ☆ Hike the Bar Island Trail during low tide
☆ ☆ ☆ ☆ ☆ Visit Bass Harbor Head Light Station
☆ ☆ ☆ ☆ ☆ Dine at the Jordan Pond House Restaurant
☆ ☆ ☆ ☆ ☆ Explore the Sieur de Monts area of the park
☆ ☆ ☆ ☆ ☆ Birdwatch along the Ship Harbor Nature Trail
☆ ☆ ☆ ☆ ☆ Learn about indigeneous culture at the Abbe Museum

MY PARK RATINGS:

ACTIVITIES	FEW				MANY
SCENERY	DULL				SPECTACULAR
PEOPLE	CROWDED				PEACEFUL
WILDLIFE	NONE				LOTS
OVERALL	NOT FOR ME				LOVED IT!

....

MOST MEMORABLE MOMENTS:

....

SPACE TO JOURNAL / DRAW / COLLECT OFFICIAL NATIONAL PARK PASSPORT STAMPS:

Arches National Park

UT

Est. 1971 — 76,679 acres — 38° 43' 59" N, 109° 35' 33" W

WHEN I VISITED:

WHO I WENT WITH:

WILDLIFE I SAW:

WHERE I STAYED:

FAVORITE EXPERIENCE:

WOULD I RETURN? yes/no

TOP 10 THINGS TO DO IN THIS PARK:

☆☆☆☆☆ Take a photo of the park's iconic Balanced Rock
☆☆☆☆☆ Catch a glimpse of the Milky Way Galaxy on a clear night
☆☆☆☆☆ Join a ranger-led guided walk through the Fiery Furnace
☆☆☆☆☆ Learn about the park's geology at Arches Visitor Center
☆☆☆☆☆ Trek through the Windows
☆☆☆☆☆ Admire Landscape Arch, the longest in North America
☆☆☆☆☆ View ancient rock art at Courthouse Wash
☆☆☆☆☆ Visit the Wolfe Ranch historic site
☆☆☆☆☆ Hike Delicate Arch Trail to the park's most famous arch
☆☆☆☆☆ Roam through the trail-less Petrified Dunes

MY PARK RATINGS:

ACTIVITIES	FEW				MANY
SCENERY	DULL				SPECTACULAR
PEOPLE	CROWDED				PEACEFUL
WILDLIFE	NONE				LOTS
OVERALL	NOT FOR ME				LOVED IT!

....

MOST MEMORABLE MOMENTS:

....

SPACE TO JOURNAL / DRAW / COLLECT OFFICIAL NATIONAL PARK PASSPORT STAMPS:

Badlands National Park

SD

Est. 1978 — 242,756 acres — 43° 37' 31" N, 102° 52' 33" W

WHEN I VISITED:

WHO I WENT WITH:

WILDLIFE I SAW:

WHERE I STAYED:

FAVORITE EXPERIENCE:

WOULD I RETURN? yes/no

TOP 10 THINGS TO DO IN THIS PARK:

☆☆☆☆☆ Take a scenic drive along Badlands Loop Road
☆☆☆☆☆ View the prairie from Pinnacles Overlook
☆☆☆☆☆ Birdwatch for herons, hawks and eagles on Castle Trail
☆☆☆☆☆ Learn about fossils on Fossil Exhibit Trail
☆☆☆☆☆ Enjoy a local meal at Cedar Pass Lodge Restaurant
☆☆☆☆☆ Observe prairie dogs at Roberts Prairie Dog Town
☆☆☆☆☆ Stargaze at the Cedar Pass Campground amphitheater
☆☆☆☆☆ Learn about the park's geology on a Ranger-led walk
☆☆☆☆☆ Hike Notch Trail to a stunning view of White River Valley
☆☆☆☆☆ View grazing bison in the Sage Creek Wilderness Area

MY PARK RATINGS:

ACTIVITIES	FEW				MANY
SCENERY	DULL				SPECTACULAR
PEOPLE	CROWDED				PEACEFUL
WILDLIFE	NONE				LOTS
OVERALL	NOT FOR ME				LOVED IT!

· ·

MOST MEMORABLE MOMENTS:

· ·

SPACE TO JOURNAL / DRAW / COLLECT OFFICIAL NATIONAL PARK PASSPORT STAMPS:

Big Bend National Park

Est. 1944 — 801,163 acres — 29° 15' 0" N, 29° 15' 0" W

WHEN I VISITED:

WHO I WENT WITH:

WILDLIFE I SAW:

WHERE I STAYED:

FAVORITE EXPERIENCE:

WOULD I RETURN? yes/no

TOP 10 THINGS TO DO IN THIS PARK:

☆☆☆☆☆ Look for wildlife on the Rio Grande Village Nature Trail
☆☆☆☆☆ Take a dip in the park's 105-degree hot springs
☆☆☆☆☆ View dinosaur fossils at the Fossil Discovery Exhibit
☆☆☆☆☆ Drive or bike the 30-mile Ross Maxwell Scenic Drive
☆☆☆☆☆ Hike to Balanced Rock on Grapevine Hills Trail
☆☆☆☆☆ Collect a passport stamp at Panther Junction Visitor Center
☆☆☆☆☆ Cross the border into Mexico and visit Boquillas del Carmen
☆☆☆☆☆ Explore the Castolon Historic District
☆☆☆☆☆ Learn about frontier life at the Sam Nail Ranch
☆☆☆☆☆ Hike Emory Peak Trail to Big Bend's highest peak

MY PARK RATINGS:

ACTIVITIES	FEW				MANY
SCENERY	DULL				SPECTACULAR
PEOPLE	CROWDED				PEACEFUL
WILDLIFE	NONE				LOTS
OVERALL	NOT FOR ME				LOVED IT!

....

MOST MEMORABLE MOMENTS:

....

SPACE TO JOURNAL / DRAW / COLLECT OFFICIAL NATIONAL PARK PASSPORT STAMPS:

Biscayne National Park

Est. 1980 — 172,971 acres — 25° 39' 0" N, 80° 4' 48" W

WHEN I VISITED:

WHO I WENT WITH:

WILDLIFE I SAW:

WHERE I STAYED:

FAVORITE EXPERIENCE:

WOULD I RETURN? yes/no

TOP 10 THINGS TO DO IN THIS PARK:

☆☆☆☆☆ Snorkel near a shipwreck on the Martime Heritage Trail
☆☆☆☆☆ Climb the Boca Chita Lighthouse
☆☆☆☆☆ Go on a Biscayne National Park Institute boat tour
☆☆☆☆☆ Watch for shorebirds at the end of Black Point Jetty
☆☆☆☆☆ Paddle a kayak or canoe down Hurricane Creek
☆☆☆☆☆ Look for rays and jellyfish in Jones Lagoon
☆☆☆☆☆ View park-inspired artwork in the visitor center art gallery
☆☆☆☆☆ Hike Elliott Key Loop Trail to the Atlantic Ocean
☆☆☆☆☆ Watch a short film at Dante Fascell Visitor Center
☆☆☆☆☆ Spot a manatee on the Mowry Canal Paddle Trail

MY PARK RATINGS:

ACTIVITIES	FEW				MANY
SCENERY	DULL				SPECTACULAR
PEOPLE	CROWDED				PEACEFUL
WILDLIFE	NONE				LOTS
OVERALL	NOT FOR ME				LOVED IT!

....

MOST MEMORABLE MOMENTS:

....

SPACE TO JOURNAL / DRAW / COLLECT OFFICIAL NATIONAL PARK PASSPORT STAMPS:

Black Canyon of the Gunnison NP

CO — Est. 1999 — 30,750 acres — 38° 34' 12" N, 107° 43' 12" W

WHEN I VISITED:

WHO I WENT WITH:

WILDLIFE I SAW:

WHERE I STAYED:

FAVORITE EXPERIENCE:

WOULD I RETURN? yes/no

TOP 10 THINGS TO DO IN THIS PARK:

- ☆☆☆☆☆ Hike North Vista Trail to the top of Green Mountain
- ☆☆☆☆☆ Chat with a ranger at the South Rim Visitor Center
- ☆☆☆☆☆ Watch the sunset from Sunset View
- ☆☆☆☆☆ View the canyon from the banks of the Gunnison River
- ☆☆☆☆☆ Drive or bike the 7-mile South Rim Road
- ☆☆☆☆☆ See Painted Wall, Colorado's tallest cliff
- ☆☆☆☆☆ Photograph one of the park's iconic twisted Juniper trees
- ☆☆☆☆☆ Hike to Exclamation Point
- ☆☆☆☆☆ Stargaze over Painted Wall from the South Rim
- ☆☆☆☆☆ Birdwatch on the North Rim's Chasm View Nature Trail

MY PARK RATINGS:

ACTIVITIES	FEW				MANY
SCENERY	DULL				SPECTACULAR
PEOPLE	CROWDED				PEACEFUL
WILDLIFE	NONE				LOTS
OVERALL	NOT FOR ME				LOVED IT!

....

MOST MEMORABLE MOMENTS:

....

SPACE TO JOURNAL / DRAW / COLLECT OFFICIAL NATIONAL PARK PASSPORT STAMPS:

Bryce Canyon National Park

UT — Est. 1924 — 35,835 acres — 37° 34' 12" N, 112° 10' 48" W

WHEN I VISITED:

WHO I WENT WITH:

WILDLIFE I SAW:

WHERE I STAYED:

FAVORITE EXPERIENCE:

WOULD I RETURN? yes/no

TOP 10 THINGS TO DO IN THIS PARK:

- ☆☆☆☆☆ Stop at all 13 viewpoints on the park's 38-mile scenic drive
- ☆☆☆☆☆ Watch the sunrise from Sunrise Point
- ☆☆☆☆☆ Attend the annual Bryce Canyon Astronomy Festival
- ☆☆☆☆☆ Hike the floor of Bryce Amphitheater on Queen's Garden Trail
- ☆☆☆☆☆ Wind through Wall Street on Navajo Loop
- ☆☆☆☆☆ Admire the stars during a ranger-led astronomy program
- ☆☆☆☆☆ Enjoy a meal at The Lodge at Bryce Canyon Restaurant
- ☆☆☆☆☆ Look for wildlife along Peek-a-Boo Loop
- ☆☆☆☆☆ Visit the waterfall at the end of Mossy Cave Trail
- ☆☆☆☆☆ Learn about the park's geology at Bryce Canyon GeoFest

MY PARK RATINGS:

ACTIVITIES	FEW				MANY
SCENERY	DULL				SPECTACULAR
PEOPLE	CROWDED				PEACEFUL
WILDLIFE	NONE				LOTS
OVERALL	NOT FOR ME				LOVED IT!

....

MOST MEMORABLE MOMENTS:

....

SPACE TO JOURNAL / DRAW / COLLECT OFFICIAL NATIONAL PARK PASSPORT STAMPS:

Canyonlands National Park

UT — Est. 1964 — 337,598 acres — 38° 12' 0" N, 109° 55' 48" W

WHEN I VISITED:

WHO I WENT WITH:

WILDLIFE I SAW:

WHERE I STAYED:

FAVORITE EXPERIENCE:

WOULD I RETURN? yes/no

TOP 10 THINGS TO DO IN THIS PARK:

- ☆☆☆☆☆ Hike the Chesler Park Loop in the Needles district
- ☆☆☆☆☆ Take a drive or bike ride on the 100-mile White Rim Road
- ☆☆☆☆☆ View petroglyphs at the Great Gallery in Horseshoe Canyon
- ☆☆☆☆☆ Watch the sunrise at the park's famed Mesa Arch
- ☆☆☆☆☆ Take a white water rafting trip on the Cataract Canyon rapids
- ☆☆☆☆☆ Admire the 360° view from Grand View Point Trail
- ☆☆☆☆☆ Go four-wheel driving in the Maze
- ☆☆☆☆☆ Visit Upheaval Dome in the Island in the Sky district
- ☆☆☆☆☆ Hike the Aztec Butte Trail to see Ancestral Pueblo dwellings
- ☆☆☆☆☆ Check out an exhibit at the Island in the Sky Visitor Center

MY PARK RATINGS:

ACTIVITIES	FEW				MANY
SCENERY	DULL				SPECTACULAR
PEOPLE	CROWDED				PEACEFUL
WILDLIFE	NONE				LOTS
OVERALL	NOT FOR ME				LOVED IT!

．．

MOST MEMORABLE MOMENTS:

．．

SPACE TO JOURNAL / DRAW / COLLECT OFFICIAL
NATIONAL PARK PASSPORT STAMPS:

Capitol Reef National Park

UT

Est. 1971 — 241,904 acres — 38° 12' 0" N, 111° 10' 12" W

WHEN I VISITED:

WHO I WENT WITH:

WILDLIFE I SAW:

WHERE I STAYED:

FAVORITE EXPERIENCE:

WOULD I RETURN? yes/no

TOP 10 THINGS TO DO IN THIS PARK:

☆☆☆☆☆ Photograph the petroglyphs in the Fruita Historic District

☆☆☆☆☆ Have a slice of locally made pie at Gifford Homestead

☆☆☆☆☆ Hike to the top of Cassidy Arch

☆☆☆☆☆ Walk along the Fremont River to Hickman Bridge

☆☆☆☆☆ Drive or bike the 7.9-mile Capitol Reef Scenic Drive

☆☆☆☆☆ Admire the breathtaking 360° view from Navajo Knobs

☆☆☆☆☆ Hike Capitol Gorge Trail to the Pioneer Register

☆☆☆☆☆ Pick fruit in the Fruita Orchards

☆☆☆☆☆ Get off the beaten path and loop the Waterpocket Fold

☆☆☆☆☆ Explore the sandstone monoliths of Cathedral Valley

MY PARK RATINGS:

ACTIVITIES	FEW				MANY
SCENERY	DULL				SPECTACULAR
PEOPLE	CROWDED				PEACEFUL
WILDLIFE	NONE				LOTS
OVERALL	NOT FOR ME				LOVED IT!

....

MOST MEMORABLE MOMENTS:

....

SPACE TO JOURNAL / DRAW / COLLECT OFFICIAL NATIONAL PARK PASSPORT STAMPS:

Carlsbad Caverns National Park

NM

Est. 1930 — 46,766 acres — 32° 10' 12" N, 104° 26' 24" W

WHEN I VISITED:

WHO I WENT WITH:

WILDLIFE I SAW:

WHERE I STAYED:

FAVORITE EXPERIENCE:

WOULD I RETURN? yes/no

TOP 10 THINGS TO DO IN THIS PARK:

- ☆☆☆☆☆ Enter the park via Natural Entrance Trail
- ☆☆☆☆☆ See the Big Room, the country's 5th largest limestone chamber
- ☆☆☆☆☆ Take a ranger-led tour through the caverns
- ☆☆☆☆☆ Look for wildlife on the 9.5-mile Walnut Canyon Desert Drive
- ☆☆☆☆☆ Relax at Rattlesnake Springs
- ☆☆☆☆☆ Watch half a million bats fly at the Bat Flight Amphitheater
- ☆☆☆☆☆ Admire the stalactites and stalagmites in the King's Palace
- ☆☆☆☆☆ Gaze into the Bottomless Pit
- ☆☆☆☆☆ Visit the Monarch in Slaughter Canyon Cave
- ☆☆☆☆☆ Venture into the Hall of the White Giant

MY PARK RATINGS:

ACTIVITIES	FEW				MANY
SCENERY	DULL				SPECTACULAR
PEOPLE	CROWDED				PEACEFUL
WILDLIFE	NONE				LOTS
OVERALL	NOT FOR ME				LOVED IT!

....

MOST MEMORABLE MOMENTS:

....

SPACE TO JOURNAL / DRAW / COLLECT OFFICIAL NATIONAL PARK PASSPORT STAMPS:

Channel Islands National Park

Est. 1980 — 249,561 acres — 34° 0' 36" N, 119° 25' 12" W

WHEN I VISITED:

WHO I WENT WITH:

WILDLIFE I SAW:

WHERE I STAYED:

FAVORITE EXPERIENCE:

WOULD I RETURN? yes/no

TOP 10 THINGS TO DO IN THIS PARK:

☆☆☆☆☆ Watch for whales and dolphins on an island ferry
☆☆☆☆☆ Take a guided kayak tour to Painted Cave
☆☆☆☆☆ Snorkel in the park's kelp forests on Anacapa Island
☆☆☆☆☆ Hike from Scorpion Beach to Smugglers Cove
☆☆☆☆☆ Spot an island fox, which are found nowhere else on Earth
☆☆☆☆☆ Observe the sea lion and seal colonies at Point Bennett
☆☆☆☆☆ Enjoy the view of East Anacapa from Inspiration Point
☆☆☆☆☆ Learn about local wildlife at the Santa Barbara Island museum
☆☆☆☆☆ Hike to Pelican Cove on Santa Cruz Island
☆☆☆☆☆ See rare Torrey pines on East Point Trail on Santa Rosa Island

MY PARK RATINGS:

ACTIVITIES	FEW				MANY
SCENERY	DULL				SPECTACULAR
PEOPLE	CROWDED				PEACEFUL
WILDLIFE	NONE				LOTS
OVERALL	NOT FOR ME				LOVED IT!

....

MOST MEMORABLE MOMENTS:

....

SPACE TO JOURNAL / DRAW / COLLECT OFFICIAL NATIONAL PARK PASSPORT STAMPS:

Congaree National Park

Est. 2003 — 26,276 acres — 33° 46' 48" N, 80° 46' 48" W

WHEN I VISITED:

WHO I WENT WITH:

WILDLIFE I SAW:

WHERE I STAYED:

FAVORITE EXPERIENCE:

WOULD I RETURN? yes/no

TOP 10 THINGS TO DO IN THIS PARK:

- ☆☆☆☆☆ Take in the scenery on the 2.6-mile Boardwalk Loop Trail
- ☆☆☆☆☆ Drift along Cedar Creek in a kayak or canoe
- ☆☆☆☆☆ Hike to Wise Lake from the Weston Lake Loop Trail
- ☆☆☆☆☆ Observe the park's famous synchronous fireflies
- ☆☆☆☆☆ Birdwatch for pileated woodpeckers along the Kingsnake Trail
- ☆☆☆☆☆ Paddle down the Congaree River on a ranger-led canoe tour
- ☆☆☆☆☆ Go fishing along the Congaree River or Cedar Creek
- ☆☆☆☆☆ Snag a souvenir from the Harry Hampton Visitor Center
- ☆☆☆☆☆ Hike to General Greene Tree, the park's largest bald cypress
- ☆☆☆☆☆ See the Congaree River from Bates Ferry Trail

MY PARK RATINGS:

ACTIVITIES	FEW				MANY
SCENERY	DULL				SPECTACULAR
PEOPLE	CROWDED				PEACEFUL
WILDLIFE	NONE				LOTS
OVERALL	NOT FOR ME				LOVED IT!

• •

MOST MEMORABLE MOMENTS:

• •

SPACE TO JOURNAL / DRAW / COLLECT OFFICIAL NATIONAL PARK PASSPORT STAMPS:

Crater Lake National Park

OR

Est. 1902 — 183,224 acres — 42° 56' 24" N, 122° 6' 0" W

WHEN I VISITED:

WHO I WENT WITH:

WILDLIFE I SAW:

WHERE I STAYED:

FAVORITE EXPERIENCE:

WOULD I RETURN? yes/no

TOP 10 THINGS TO DO IN THIS PARK:

- ☆☆☆☆☆ Drive or bike the 33-mile Rim Drive around Crater Lake
- ☆☆☆☆☆ View the park's stunning spires from Pinnacles Overlook
- ☆☆☆☆☆ Enjoy a meal at the Crater Lake Lodge Dining Room
- ☆☆☆☆☆ Admire the view from Sinnott Memorial Overlook
- ☆☆☆☆☆ Collect an official passport stamp from Rim Visitor Center
- ☆☆☆☆☆ Hike Wizard Island Summit Trail to the cinder cone's peak
- ☆☆☆☆☆ Take a ranger-led trolley tour of the Rim Drive
- ☆☆☆☆☆ Watch the sunset over the lake from Watchman Overlook
- ☆☆☆☆☆ Swim in Crater Lake at the end of Cleetwood Cove Trail
- ☆☆☆☆☆ Stroll along the picturesque Castle Crest Wildflower Trail

MY PARK RATINGS:

ACTIVITIES	FEW				MANY
SCENERY	DULL				SPECTACULAR
PEOPLE	CROWDED				PEACEFUL
WILDLIFE	NONE				LOTS
OVERALL	NOT FOR ME				LOVED IT!

....

MOST MEMORABLE MOMENTS:

....

SPACE TO JOURNAL / DRAW / COLLECT OFFICIAL NATIONAL PARK PASSPORT STAMPS:

Cuyahoga Valley National Park

OH — Est. 2000 — 32,571 acres — 41° 14' 24" N, 81° 33' 0" W

WHEN I VISITED:

WHO I WENT WITH:

WILDLIFE I SAW:

WHERE I STAYED:

FAVORITE EXPERIENCE:

WOULD I RETURN? yes/no

TOP 10 THINGS TO DO IN THIS PARK:

- ☆☆☆☆☆ Hike to Brandywine Falls, the park's 65-foot waterfall
- ☆☆☆☆☆ Look for beavers, muskrats, turtles and more at Beaver Marsh
- ☆☆☆☆☆ Hike or cross country ski the Tree Farm Trail
- ☆☆☆☆☆ Learn some Cuyahoga Valley history at Hale Farm
- ☆☆☆☆☆ Ride the Cuyahoga Valley Scenic Railroad
- ☆☆☆☆☆ Explore the Cuyahoga River by canoe or kayak
- ☆☆☆☆☆ Photograph Everett Covered Bridge
- ☆☆☆☆☆ Learn about the Ohio & Erie Canal at the Exploration Center
- ☆☆☆☆☆ Take in the spectacular views from Ledges Overlook Trail
- ☆☆☆☆☆ Complete a quest from Boston Mill Visitor Center

MY PARK RATINGS:

ACTIVITIES	FEW				MANY
SCENERY	DULL				SPECTACULAR
PEOPLE	CROWDED				PEACEFUL
WILDLIFE	NONE				LOTS
OVERALL	NOT FOR ME				LOVED IT!

....

MOST MEMORABLE MOMENTS:

....

SPACE TO JOURNAL / DRAW / COLLECT OFFICIAL NATIONAL PARK PASSPORT STAMPS:

Death Valley National Park

Est. 1994 — 3.4 million acres — 36° 14' 24" N, 116° 49' 12" W

WHEN I VISITED:

WHO I WENT WITH:

WILDLIFE I SAW:

WHERE I STAYED:

FAVORITE EXPERIENCE:

WOULD I RETURN? yes/no

TOP 10 THINGS TO DO IN THIS PARK:

☆☆☆☆☆ Hike into Badwater Basin, the lowest point in North America

☆☆☆☆☆ Watch the sunset from Zabriskie Point

☆☆☆☆☆ Stop at Artist's Palette on the 9-mile Artists Drive

☆☆☆☆☆ Visit the remnants of the historic Keane Wonder Mine

☆☆☆☆☆ View the famous sailing stones in Racetrack Playa

☆☆☆☆☆ Check out the Wildrose Charcoal Kilns

☆☆☆☆☆ Overlook the heart of Death Valley from Dante's View

☆☆☆☆☆ Hike to Darwin Falls, the park's year-round waterfall

☆☆☆☆☆ Gaze up at the night sky from Harmony Borax Works

☆☆☆☆☆ Sled down the Mesquite Flat or Eureka Sand Dunes

MY PARK RATINGS:

ACTIVITIES	FEW				MANY
SCENERY	DULL				SPECTACULAR
PEOPLE	CROWDED				PEACEFUL
WILDLIFE	NONE				LOTS
OVERALL	NOT FOR ME				LOVED IT!

· ·

MOST MEMORABLE MOMENTS:

· ·

SPACE TO JOURNAL / DRAW / COLLECT OFFICIAL
NATIONAL PARK PASSPORT STAMPS:

Denali National Park

Est. 1917 — 6.1 million acres — 63° 19' 48" N, 150° 30' 0" W

WHEN I VISITED:

WHO I WENT WITH:

WILDLIFE I SAW:

WHERE I STAYED:

FAVORITE EXPERIENCE:

WOULD I RETURN? yes/no

TOP 10 THINGS TO DO IN THIS PARK:

- ☆☆☆☆☆ Meet the park's sled dogs at the country's oldest dogsled kennel
- ☆☆☆☆☆ Hop on the Kantishna Experience narrated bus tour
- ☆☆☆☆☆ Admire the breathtaking view from Polychrome Overlook
- ☆☆☆☆☆ Photograph Denali from Stony Hill Overlook
- ☆☆☆☆☆ Spend the night in a backcountry lodge in Kantishna
- ☆☆☆☆☆ Spot Alaska's Big 5 (moose, bear, wolf, caribou & Dall sheep)
- ☆☆☆☆☆ Hike Thorofare Ridge Trail for jaw-dropping views of Denali
- ☆☆☆☆☆ View the park from above on a flightseeing tour
- ☆☆☆☆☆ Collect an official park passport stamp at Denali Visitor Center
- ☆☆☆☆☆ Check out park-inspired art at Eielson Visitor Center

MY PARK RATINGS:

ACTIVITIES	FEW				MANY
SCENERY	DULL				SPECTACULAR
PEOPLE	CROWDED				PEACEFUL
WILDLIFE	NONE				LOTS
OVERALL	NOT FOR ME				LOVED IT!

....

MOST MEMORABLE MOMENTS:

....

SPACE TO JOURNAL / DRAW / COLLECT OFFICIAL NATIONAL PARK PASSPORT STAMPS:

Dry Tortugas National Park
Est. 1992 — 64,701 acres — 24° 37' 48" N, 82° 52' 12" W

WHEN I VISITED:

WHO I WENT WITH:

WILDLIFE I SAW:

WHERE I STAYED:

FAVORITE EXPERIENCE:

WOULD I RETURN? yes/no

TOP 10 THINGS TO DO IN THIS PARK:

☆ ☆ ☆ ☆ ☆ Go snorkeling in the crystal clear waters of Dry Tortugas
☆ ☆ ☆ ☆ ☆ Walk to the remote East Beach at the end of Bush Key
☆ ☆ ☆ ☆ ☆ Embark on a guided tour of Fort Jefferson
☆ ☆ ☆ ☆ ☆ View the sooty terns at Bush Key, their only U.S. nesting site
☆ ☆ ☆ ☆ ☆ Check out the artifacts inside Garden Key Visitor Center
☆ ☆ ☆ ☆ ☆ Take a boat to the secluded Loggerhead Key Beach
☆ ☆ ☆ ☆ ☆ Watch the sunset over South Beach on Garden Key
☆ ☆ ☆ ☆ ☆ See the Tortugas Harbor Lighthouse
☆ ☆ ☆ ☆ ☆ Stroll the white sands of North Beach on Garden Key
☆ ☆ ☆ ☆ ☆ Look for squid, nurse sharks and barracude at the Moat Wall

MY PARK RATINGS:

ACTIVITIES	FEW				MANY
SCENERY	DULL				SPECTACULAR
PEOPLE	CROWDED				PEACEFUL
WILDLIFE	NONE				LOTS
OVERALL	NOT FOR ME				LOVED IT!

• •

MOST MEMORABLE MOMENTS:

• •

SPACE TO JOURNAL / DRAW / COLLECT OFFICIAL NATIONAL PARK PASSPORT STAMPS:

Everglades National Park

Est. 1947 — 1.5 million acres — 25° 19' 12" N, 80° 55' 48" W

WHEN I VISITED:

WHO I WENT WITH:

WILDLIFE I SAW:

WHERE I STAYED:

FAVORITE EXPERIENCE:

WOULD I RETURN? yes/no

TOP 10 THINGS TO DO IN THIS PARK:

☆☆☆☆☆ View America's largest mahogany tree in Mahogany Hammock
☆☆☆☆☆ Admire the landscape from Pa-hay-okee Lookout Tower
☆☆☆☆☆ Spot an alligator while hiking the short Anhinga Trail
☆☆☆☆☆ Watch a film about the park at Ernest F. Coe Visitor Center
☆☆☆☆☆ Paddle the Nine Mile Pond Trail in a kayak or canoe
☆☆☆☆☆ Tour Shark Valley by tram
☆☆☆☆☆ Take a ranger-led tour of the historic Nike Missile Site
☆☆☆☆☆ Climb to the top of Shark Valley Observation Tower
☆☆☆☆☆ Watch wading birds feed at Mrazek Pond or Coot Bay Pond
☆☆☆☆☆ Enjoy the 38-mile scenic drive along State Road 9336

MY PARK RATINGS:

ACTIVITIES	FEW				MANY
SCENERY	DULL				SPECTACULAR
PEOPLE	CROWDED				PEACEFUL
WILDLIFE	NONE				LOTS
OVERALL	NOT FOR ME				LOVED IT!

. . . .

MOST MEMORABLE MOMENTS:

. . . .

SPACE TO JOURNAL / DRAW / COLLECT OFFICIAL NATIONAL PARK PASSPORT STAMPS:

Gates of the Arctic National Park

Est. 1980 — 8.5 million acres — 67° 46' 48" N, 153° 18' 0" W

WHEN I VISITED:

WHO I WENT WITH:

WILDLIFE I SAW:

WHERE I STAYED:

FAVORITE EXPERIENCE:

WOULD I RETURN? yes/no

TOP 10 THINGS TO DO IN THIS PARK:

- ☆☆☆☆☆ Photograph the Arrigetch Peaks, a National Natural Landmark
- ☆☆☆☆☆ Visit Walker Lake, another National Natural Landmark
- ☆☆☆☆☆ Explore the nearby Nunamuit Inupiaq village of Anaktuvuk Pass
- ☆☆☆☆☆ Backpack or packraft into a remote area of the park
- ☆☆☆☆☆ Chat with a ranger at the Anaktuvuk Pass Ranger Station
- ☆☆☆☆☆ Watch a film at the Alaska Public Lands Info Center
- ☆☆☆☆☆ Hike to the glacial blue lakes of Aquarius Valley
- ☆☆☆☆☆ Take a rafting trip down one of the park's wild and scenic rivers
- ☆☆☆☆☆ Catch a glimpse of caribou or grizzly bears
- ☆☆☆☆☆ Collect an official park stamp from the Bettles Ranger Station

MY PARK RATINGS:

ACTIVITIES	FEW				MANY
SCENERY	DULL				SPECTACULAR
PEOPLE	CROWDED				PEACEFUL
WILDLIFE	NONE				LOTS
OVERALL	NOT FOR ME				LOVED IT!

....

MOST MEMORABLE MOMENTS:

....

SPACE TO JOURNAL / DRAW / COLLECT OFFICIAL NATIONAL PARK PASSPORT STAMPS:

Gateway Arch National Park

MO — Est. 2018 — 193 acres — 38° 37' 48" N, 90° 11' 24" W

WHEN I VISITED:

WHO I WENT WITH:

WILDLIFE I SAW:

WHERE I STAYED:

FAVORITE EXPERIENCE:

WOULD I RETURN? yes/no

TOP 10 THINGS TO DO IN THIS PARK:

- ☆☆☆☆☆ Ride the tram to the top of Gateway Arch
- ☆☆☆☆☆ Learn about the park at the interactive Gateway Arch Museum
- ☆☆☆☆☆ Travel back in time on a Mississippi River riverboat cruise
- ☆☆☆☆☆ Check out the civil rights exhibits at the Old Courthouse
- ☆☆☆☆☆ Watch the Monument to the Dream film at Tucker Theater
- ☆☆☆☆☆ Collect an official park stamp at Gateway Arch Visitor Center
- ☆☆☆☆☆ Visit the Explorers' Garden in North Gateway
- ☆☆☆☆☆ View the Gateway Arch from above on a helicopter tour
- ☆☆☆☆☆ Grab a snack at the Arch Cafe inside the visitor center
- ☆☆☆☆☆ Walk alongside the Mississippi River on the park's paved trails

MY PARK RATINGS:

ACTIVITIES	FEW				MANY
SCENERY	DULL				SPECTACULAR
PEOPLE	CROWDED				PEACEFUL
WILDLIFE	NONE				LOTS
OVERALL	NOT FOR ME				LOVED IT!

. . . .

MOST MEMORABLE MOMENTS:

. . . .

SPACE TO JOURNAL / DRAW / COLLECT OFFICIAL NATIONAL PARK PASSPORT STAMPS:

Glacier National Park

MT

Est. 1910 — 1 million acres — 48° 48' 0" N, 114° 0' 0" W

WHEN I VISITED:

WHO I WENT WITH:

WILDLIFE I SAW:

WHERE I STAYED:

FAVORITE EXPERIENCE:

WOULD I RETURN? yes/no

TOP 10 THINGS TO DO IN THIS PARK:

- ☆☆☆☆☆ Drive or bike the scenic 50-mile Going-to-the-Sun Road
- ☆☆☆☆☆ Look for bighorn sheep and mountain goats at Logan Pass
- ☆☆☆☆☆ Hike through the Hanging Gardens to Hidden Lake Overlook
- ☆☆☆☆☆ Take a Red Bus tour through Many Glacier or Two Medicine
- ☆☆☆☆☆ Hike from Swiftcurrent Lake to Grinnell Glacier
- ☆☆☆☆☆ Stop and smell the wildflowers on Highline Trail
- ☆☆☆☆☆ Take a guided boat tour of Avalanche Lake or Lake McDonald
- ☆☆☆☆☆ See Wild Goose Island on St. Mary Lake
- ☆☆☆☆☆ Visit Avalanche Gorge by way of the Trail of the Cedars
- ☆☆☆☆☆ Cross the border into Canada on a boat tour of Waterton Lake

MY PARK RATINGS:

ACTIVITIES	FEW				MANY
SCENERY	DULL				SPECTACULAR
PEOPLE	CROWDED				PEACEFUL
WILDLIFE	NONE				LOTS
OVERALL	NOT FOR ME				LOVED IT!

....

MOST MEMORABLE MOMENTS:

....

SPACE TO JOURNAL / DRAW / COLLECT OFFICIAL NATIONAL PARK PASSPORT STAMPS:

Glacier Bay National Park

Est. 1980 — 3.3 million acres — 58° 30' 0" N, 137° 0' 0" W

WHEN I VISITED:

WHO I WENT WITH:

WILDLIFE I SAW:

WHERE I STAYED:

FAVORITE EXPERIENCE:

WOULD I RETURN? yes/no

TOP 10 THINGS TO DO IN THIS PARK:

- ☆☆☆☆☆ Sail to Marjorie Glacier on the Glacier Bay Day Boat
- ☆☆☆☆☆ Learn about indigenous Tlingit culture at the Huna Tribal House
- ☆☆☆☆☆ See the humpback whale skeleton on Tlingit Trail
- ☆☆☆☆☆ Watch the Beneath the Reflections film at the Visitor Center
- ☆☆☆☆☆ Dine at the Fairweather Dining Room at Glacier Bay Lodge
- ☆☆☆☆☆ Birdwatch for puffins near South Marble Island
- ☆☆☆☆☆ Watch bears fish for Alaskan salmon on Bartlett River Trail
- ☆☆☆☆☆ Chat with a ranger at the Visitor Information Station
- ☆☆☆☆☆ Look for whales on a guided kayak tour of Point Adolphus
- ☆☆☆☆☆ See the Juneau Icefield from above on a flightseeing tour

MY PARK RATINGS:

ACTIVITIES	FEW				MANY
SCENERY	DULL				SPECTACULAR
PEOPLE	CROWDED				PEACEFUL
WILDLIFE	NONE				LOTS
OVERALL	NOT FOR ME				LOVED IT!

....

MOST MEMORABLE MOMENTS:

....

SPACE TO JOURNAL / DRAW / COLLECT OFFICIAL NATIONAL PARK PASSPORT STAMPS:

Grand Canyon National Park

AZ

Est. 1919 — 1.2 million acres — 36° 3' 36" N, 112° 8' 24" W

WHEN I VISITED:

WHO I WENT WITH:

WILDLIFE I SAW:

WHERE I STAYED:

FAVORITE EXPERIENCE:

WOULD I RETURN? yes/no

TOP 10 THINGS TO DO IN THIS PARK:

☆☆☆☆☆ Hike to the bottom of the canyon on Bright Angel Trail
☆☆☆☆☆ Take in the panoramic views from Desert View Watchtower
☆☆☆☆☆ Locate the Mather Plaque at Mather Point
☆☆☆☆☆ Visit the Skywalk on the Hualapai Indian Reservation
☆☆☆☆☆ Ride the free shuttle bus along the 7-mile Hermit Road
☆☆☆☆☆ Take a guided mule ride into the canyon
☆☆☆☆☆ See the 800-year-old ancestral Pueblan village at Tusayan Ruin
☆☆☆☆☆ Learn about the land at the Yavapai Museum of Geology
☆☆☆☆☆ Watch for elk along the 25-mile scenic Desert View Drive
☆☆☆☆☆ Look down at the Colorado River from Hopi Point

MY PARK RATINGS:

ACTIVITIES	FEW				MANY
SCENERY	DULL				SPECTACULAR
PEOPLE	CROWDED				PEACEFUL
WILDLIFE	NONE				LOTS
OVERALL	NOT FOR ME				LOVED IT!

....

MOST MEMORABLE MOMENTS:

....

SPACE TO JOURNAL / DRAW / COLLECT OFFICIAL NATIONAL PARK PASSPORT STAMPS:

Grand Teton National Park

WY

Est. 1929 — 310,044 acres — 43° 43' 48" N, 110° 48' 0" W

WHEN I VISITED:

WHO I WENT WITH:

WILDLIFE I SAW:

WHERE I STAYED:

FAVORITE EXPERIENCE:

WOULD I RETURN? yes/no

TOP 10 THINGS TO DO IN THIS PARK:

☆☆☆☆☆ Hike Phelps Lake Overlook Trail for a stunning view of the lake
☆☆☆☆☆ View the Teton range along the 42-mile Scenic Drive
☆☆☆☆☆ Explore the 1890s homestead of Mormon Row Historic Area
☆☆☆☆☆ Stop by the Laurance S. Rockefeller Preserve Center
☆☆☆☆☆ Make the 1/2-mile climb to the Hidden Falls waterfall
☆☆☆☆☆ Paddle a canoe or kayak across Jackson Lake or Jenny Lake
☆☆☆☆☆ Admire the panoramic views from Signal Mountain Summit
☆☆☆☆☆ Photograph the mountain range from Schwabacher Landing
☆☆☆☆☆ Look for wildlife at sunrise at Oxbow Bend
☆☆☆☆☆ Enjoy a locally sourced meal at Jenny Lake Lodge Dining Room

MY PARK RATINGS:

ACTIVITIES	FEW				MANY
SCENERY	DULL				SPECTACULAR
PEOPLE	CROWDED				PEACEFUL
WILDLIFE	NONE				LOTS
OVERALL	NOT FOR ME				LOVED IT!

....

MOST MEMORABLE MOMENTS:

....

SPACE TO JOURNAL / DRAW / COLLECT OFFICIAL NATIONAL PARK PASSPORT STAMPS:

Great Basin National Park

Est. 1986 — 77,180 acres — 38° 58' 48" N, 114° 18' 0" W

WHEN I VISITED:

WHO I WENT WITH:

WILDLIFE I SAW:

WHERE I STAYED:

FAVORITE EXPERIENCE:

WOULD I RETURN? yes/no

TOP 10 THINGS TO DO IN THIS PARK:

- ☆☆☆☆☆ Take a ranger-led tour of the park's famous Lehman Caves
- ☆☆☆☆☆ Drive or bike the 24-mile Wheeler Peak Scenic Drive
- ☆☆☆☆☆ View the black-and-white photos inside Rhodes Cabin
- ☆☆☆☆☆ Look for wildlife along the gravel Baker Creek Road
- ☆☆☆☆☆ Enjoy breakfast or lunch at Lehman Caves Cafe
- ☆☆☆☆☆ Stargaze with park rangers on a clear night
- ☆☆☆☆☆ Photograph the twisted ancient trees on Bristlecone Pine Trail
- ☆☆☆☆☆ Gather up to three gunnysacks of pinyon pine nuts
- ☆☆☆☆☆ Learn about park flora on Mountain View Nature Trail
- ☆☆☆☆☆ Collect an official passport stamp at Great Basin Visitor Center

MY PARK RATINGS:

ACTIVITIES	FEW				MANY
SCENERY	DULL				SPECTACULAR
PEOPLE	CROWDED				PEACEFUL
WILDLIFE	NONE				LOTS
OVERALL	NOT FOR ME				LOVED IT!

....

MOST MEMORABLE MOMENTS:

....

SPACE TO JOURNAL / DRAW / COLLECT OFFICIAL NATIONAL PARK PASSPORT STAMPS:

Great Sand Dunes National Park

CO

Est. 2004 — 107,302 acres — 37° 43' 48" N, 105° 30' 36" W

WHEN I VISITED:

WHO I WENT WITH:

WILDLIFE I SAW:

WHERE I STAYED:

FAVORITE EXPERIENCE:

WOULD I RETURN? yes/no

TOP 10 THINGS TO DO IN THIS PARK:

☆☆☆☆☆ Climb Star Dune, the tallest sand dune in North America
☆☆☆☆☆ Take in the panoramic view from the top of High Dune
☆☆☆☆☆ Sled or sanboard in the park's 30-square-mile dunefield
☆☆☆☆☆ Drive or bike the 22-mile Medano Pass Primitive Road
☆☆☆☆☆ Catch a glimpse of the Milky Way Galaxy on a clear night
☆☆☆☆☆ Listen for songbirds and hooting owls on Mosca Pass Trail
☆☆☆☆☆ See park-insipired artwork at Great Sand Dunes Visitor Center
☆☆☆☆☆ Look for elk and bison in the park's Southern Grasslands
☆☆☆☆☆ Dip your toes in Colorado's only natural beach in the wetlands
☆☆☆☆☆ Pitch a tent in the dunes with a backcountry camping permit

MY PARK RATINGS:

ACTIVITIES	FEW				MANY
SCENERY	DULL				SPECTACULAR
PEOPLE	CROWDED				PEACEFUL
WILDLIFE	NONE				LOTS
OVERALL	NOT FOR ME				LOVED IT!

· ·

MOST MEMORABLE MOMENTS:

· ·

SPACE TO JOURNAL / DRAW / COLLECT OFFICIAL NATIONAL PARK PASSPORT STAMPS:

Great Smoky Mountains NP

Est. 1934 — 522.427 acres — 35° 40' 48" N, 83° 31' 4" W

WHEN I VISITED:

WHO I WENT WITH:

WILDLIFE I SAW:

WHERE I STAYED:

FAVORITE EXPERIENCE:

WOULD I RETURN? yes/no

TOP 10 THINGS TO DO IN THIS PARK:

☆☆☆☆☆ Watch the sunrise from the peak of Mount Cammerer
☆☆☆☆☆ Look for wildlife along the 11-mile Cades Cove Loop Road
☆☆☆☆☆ Hike part of the famed Appalachian Trail
☆☆☆☆☆ Straddle the state line between North Carolina and Tennessee
☆☆☆☆☆ Enjoy the 360° view from Clingmans Dome Observation Tower
☆☆☆☆☆ Hike Abrams Falls Trail to one of the park's beautiful waterfalls
☆☆☆☆☆ Explore Elkmont Historic District's recently restored buildings
☆☆☆☆☆ Admire the Smokies from Newfound Gap Overlook
☆☆☆☆☆ Drive or bike the 6-mile Roaring Fork Motor Nature Trail
☆☆☆☆☆ Learn some Appalachian history at Mountain Farm Museum

MY PARK RATINGS:

ACTIVITIES	FEW				MANY
SCENERY	DULL				SPECTACULAR
PEOPLE	CROWDED				PEACEFUL
WILDLIFE	NONE				LOTS
OVERALL	NOT FOR ME				LOVED IT!

....

MOST MEMORABLE MOMENTS:

....

SPACE TO JOURNAL / DRAW / COLLECT OFFICIAL NATIONAL PARK PASSPORT STAMPS:

Guadalupe Mountains NP

TX — Est. 1972 — 86,367 acres — 31° 55' 12" N, 104° 52' 12" W

WHEN I VISITED:

WHO I WENT WITH:

WILDLIFE I SAW:

WHERE I STAYED:

FAVORITE EXPERIENCE:

WOULD I RETURN? yes/no

TOP 10 THINGS TO DO IN THIS PARK:

- ☆☆☆☆☆ Traverse multiple ecosystems on Guadalupe Peak Trail
- ☆☆☆☆☆ Learn about early ranch life at Frijole Ranch History Museum
- ☆☆☆☆☆ Hike to the mountaintop valley known as The Bowl
- ☆☆☆☆☆ Explore the narrow 10-foot-wide canyon on Devil's Hall Trail
- ☆☆☆☆☆ Check out the exhibits at Pine Springs Visitor Center
- ☆☆☆☆☆ Visit Pratt Cabin and the Grotto in McKittrick Canyon
- ☆☆☆☆☆ See the illustrations at McKittrick Canyon Contact Station
- ☆☆☆☆☆ Look for mule deer along Indian Meadow Nature Trail
- ☆☆☆☆☆ View the park's white salt flat from Salt Basin Overlook Trail
- ☆☆☆☆☆ Birdwatch for more than 300 species at Manzanita Springs

MY PARK RATINGS:

ACTIVITIES	FEW				MANY
SCENERY	DULL				SPECTACULAR
PEOPLE	CROWDED				PEACEFUL
WILDLIFE	NONE				LOTS
OVERALL	NOT FOR ME				LOVED IT!

....

MOST MEMORABLE MOMENTS:

....

SPACE TO JOURNAL / DRAW / COLLECT OFFICIAL NATIONAL PARK PASSPORT STAMPS:

Haleakala National Park

Est. 1916 — 33,265 acres — 20° 43' 12" N, 156° 10' 12" W

WHEN I VISITED:

WHO I WENT WITH:

WILDLIFE I SAW:

WHERE I STAYED:

FAVORITE EXPERIENCE:

WOULD I RETURN? yes/no

TOP 10 THINGS TO DO IN THIS PARK:

- ☆☆☆☆☆ Watch the sunrise above the clouds from Puu Ulaula (Red Hill)
- ☆☆☆☆☆ Hike Keoneheehee (Sliding Sands) Trail into Haleakala Crater
- ☆☆☆☆☆ See the endangered Ahinahina (Silverswords) plants
- ☆☆☆☆☆ Stargaze from Puu Ulaula or one of the visitor centers
- ☆☆☆☆☆ View the crater from the Pa Ka'oao or Kalahaku Overlooks
- ☆☆☆☆☆ Look for nene, endangered native geese, in Hosmer Grove
- ☆☆☆☆☆ Hike to the beautiful Waimoku Falls on Pipiwai Trail
- ☆☆☆☆☆ Dip your toes in the cascading waters of Oheo Gulch
- ☆☆☆☆☆ Learn about Hawaiian culture at Park HQ Visitor Center
- ☆☆☆☆☆ Admire traditional Hawaiian architecture at Hale Halawai

MY PARK RATINGS:

ACTIVITIES	FEW				MANY
SCENERY	DULL				SPECTACULAR
PEOPLE	CROWDED				PEACEFUL
WILDLIFE	NONE				LOTS
OVERALL	NOT FOR ME				LOVED IT!

....

MOST MEMORABLE MOMENTS:

....

SPACE TO JOURNAL / DRAW / COLLECT OFFICIAL NATIONAL PARK PASSPORT STAMPS:

Hawai'i Volcanoes National Park

HI

Est. 1916 — 323,431 acres — 19° 22' 48" N, 155° 12' 0" W

WHEN I VISITED:

WHO I WENT WITH:

WILDLIFE I SAW:

WHERE I STAYED:

FAVORITE EXPERIENCE:

WOULD I RETURN? yes/no

TOP 10 THINGS TO DO IN THIS PARK:

☆☆☆☆☆ Witness molten lava flowing from an active volcano

☆☆☆☆☆ Drive or bike the 19-mile Chain of Craters Road

☆☆☆☆☆ Watch a traditional hula show at Volcano Art Center

☆☆☆☆☆ View Halemaumau Crater from Steaming Bluff Overlook

☆☆☆☆☆ See the park's billowing steam vents and smelly sulphur banks

☆☆☆☆☆ Hike across a solidified lava lake on Kilauea Iki Trail

☆☆☆☆☆ Stroll through Nahuku, also known as the Thurston Lava Tube

☆☆☆☆☆ Admire the Kilauea Caldera from Kilauea Overlook

☆☆☆☆☆ Watch a documentary about the park at Kilauea Visitor Center

☆☆☆☆☆ Enjoy a meal at Volcano House, Hawai'i's oldest hotel

MY PARK RATINGS:

ACTIVITIES	FEW				MANY
SCENERY	DULL				SPECTACULAR
PEOPLE	CROWDED				PEACEFUL
WILDLIFE	NONE				LOTS
OVERALL	NOT FOR ME				LOVED IT!

· ·

MOST MEMORABLE MOMENTS:

· ·

SPACE TO JOURNAL / DRAW / COLLECT OFFICIAL NATIONAL PARK PASSPORT STAMPS:

Hot Springs National Park

AR — Est. 1921 — 5,549 acres — 34° 30' 36" N, 93° 3' 0" W

WHEN I VISITED:

WHO I WENT WITH:

WILDLIFE I SAW:

WHERE I STAYED:

FAVORITE EXPERIENCE:

WOULD I RETURN? yes/no

TOP 10 THINGS TO DO IN THIS PARK:

- ☆☆☆☆☆ Explore Bathhouse Row's eight bathhouses
- ☆☆☆☆☆ Feel the temperature of the hot springs at Hot Water Cascade
- ☆☆☆☆☆ Soak in the thermal water at Quapaw or Buckstaff Bathhouse
- ☆☆☆☆☆ Admire the 360° view from Hot Springs Mountain Tower
- ☆☆☆☆☆ Drink spring water from one of the public fountains
- ☆☆☆☆☆ Take a stroll on the Grand Promenade
- ☆☆☆☆☆ Enjoy a locally made beer at Superior Bathhouse Brewery
- ☆☆☆☆☆ Learn some park history on a trolley tour
- ☆☆☆☆☆ Join a ranger-led guided tour of Fordyce Bathhouse
- ☆☆☆☆☆ Hike Goat Rock Trail to the boulder's scenic lookout

MY PARK RATINGS:

ACTIVITIES	FEW				MANY
SCENERY	DULL				SPECTACULAR
PEOPLE	CROWDED				PEACEFUL
WILDLIFE	NONE				LOTS
OVERALL	NOT FOR ME				LOVED IT!

··

MOST MEMORABLE MOMENTS:

··

SPACE TO JOURNAL / DRAW / COLLECT OFFICIAL NATIONAL PARK PASSPORT STAMPS:

Indiana Dunes National Park

Est. 2019 — 15,347 acres — 41° 39' 11" N, 87° 3' 8" W

WHEN I VISITED:

WHO I WENT WITH:

WILDLIFE I SAW:

WHERE I STAYED:

FAVORITE EXPERIENCE:

WOULD I RETURN? yes/no

TOP 10 THINGS TO DO IN THIS PARK:

☆☆☆☆☆ Swim in Lake Michigan at one of the park's eight beaches
☆☆☆☆☆ Stroll along the 15-mile Lake Michigan shoreline
☆☆☆☆☆ Watch a film at Indiana Dunes Visitor Center
☆☆☆☆☆ Complete the Three Dune Challenge
☆☆☆☆☆ Learn about the dunes on West Dune Beach Succession Trail
☆☆☆☆☆ Climb Mount Baldy on a ranger-led hike
☆☆☆☆☆ Enjoy a lakeside picnic at Portage Lakefront and Riverwalk
☆☆☆☆☆ Visit the Bailly Homestead and Chellberg Farm
☆☆☆☆☆ Explore one of the park's rare black oak savannas
☆☆☆☆☆ Birdwatch among the wildflowers on Heron Rookery Trail

MY PARK RATINGS:

ACTIVITIES | FEW | | | | MANY

SCENERY | DULL | | | | SPECTACULAR

PEOPLE | CROWDED | | | | PEACEFUL

WILDLIFE | NONE | | | | LOTS

OVERALL | NOT FOR ME | | | | LOVED IT!

· ·

MOST MEMORABLE MOMENTS:

· ·

SPACE TO JOURNAL / DRAW / COLLECT OFFICIAL NATIONAL PARK PASSPORT STAMPS:

Isle Royale National Park

Est. 1931 — 571,790 acres — 48° 6' 0" N, 88° 33' 0" W

WHEN I VISITED:

WHO I WENT WITH:

WILDLIFE I SAW:

WHERE I STAYED:

FAVORITE EXPERIENCE:

WOULD I RETURN? yes/no

TOP 10 THINGS TO DO IN THIS PARK:

- ☆☆☆☆☆ Learn about the park's history at Rock Harbor Lighthouse
- ☆☆☆☆☆ Enjoy the panoramic view from Lookout Louise
- ☆☆☆☆☆ Traverse part of the 42-mile Greenstone Ridge Trail
- ☆☆☆☆☆ Spend a night at Rock Harbor Lodge, the park's sole hotel
- ☆☆☆☆☆ Visit Smithwick Mine on Stoll Memorial Trail
- ☆☆☆☆☆ Birdwatch for loons and peregrine falcons on Siskiwit Lake
- ☆☆☆☆☆ See the inland sea arch known as Suzy's Cave
- ☆☆☆☆☆ Collect an official park stamp at Houghton Visitor Center
- ☆☆☆☆☆ View the park from above on a scenic flightseeing tour
- ☆☆☆☆☆ Take the Rock Harbor Lodge's guided boat tour

MY PARK RATINGS:

ACTIVITIES	FEW				MANY
SCENERY	DULL				SPECTACULAR
PEOPLE	CROWDED				PEACEFUL
WILDLIFE	NONE				LOTS
OVERALL	NOT FOR ME				LOVED IT!

....

MOST MEMORABLE MOMENTS:

....

SPACE TO JOURNAL / DRAW / COLLECT OFFICIAL NATIONAL PARK PASSPORT STAMPS:

Joshua Tree National Park

Est. 1994 — 790,636 acres — 33° 47' 24" N, 115° 54' 0" W

WHEN I VISITED:

WHO I WENT WITH:

WILDLIFE I SAW:

WHERE I STAYED:

FAVORITE EXPERIENCE:

WOULD I RETURN? yes/no

TOP 10 THINGS TO DO IN THIS PARK:

- ☆☆☆☆☆ Enjoy panoramic views from the top of Ryan Mounain
- ☆☆☆☆☆ Go four-wheel driving on Geology Tour Road
- ☆☆☆☆☆ Take a guided walking tour of the 150-acre historic Keys Ranch
- ☆☆☆☆☆ Hike the short and scenic Hidden Valley Nature Trail
- ☆☆☆☆☆ Traverse the park's most scenic locales on Park Boulevard
- ☆☆☆☆☆ Stargaze on Skull Rock Nature Trail or near Arch Rock
- ☆☆☆☆☆ See the aptly nicknamed Teddy Bear Cacti at Cholla Garden
- ☆☆☆☆☆ Look for elusive bighorn sheep at Barker Dam
- ☆☆☆☆☆ View the Santa Rosa Mountains from Keys View
- ☆☆☆☆☆ Attend one of The Desert Institute's classes or field trips

MY PARK RATINGS:

ACTIVITIES	FEW				MANY
SCENERY	DULL				SPECTACULAR
PEOPLE	CROWDED				PEACEFUL
WILDLIFE	NONE				LOTS
OVERALL	NOT FOR ME				LOVED IT!

....

MOST MEMORABLE MOMENTS:

....

SPACE TO JOURNAL / DRAW / COLLECT OFFICIAL NATIONAL PARK PASSPORT STAMPS:

Katmai National Park

Est. 1980 — 4.1 million acres — 58° 30' 0" N, 155° 0' 0" W

WHEN I VISITED:

WHO I WENT WITH:

WILDLIFE I SAW:

WHERE I STAYED:

FAVORITE EXPERIENCE:

WOULD I RETURN? yes/no

TOP 10 THINGS TO DO IN THIS PARK:

☆☆☆☆☆ Take a ranger-led bus tour of the Valley of Ten Thousand Smokes

☆☆☆☆☆ Watch grizzly bears fish for salmon at the McNeil River falls

☆☆☆☆☆ Go rafting on American, Moraine or Funnel Creeks

☆☆☆☆☆ Join a ranger-led walking tour of the Brooks River area

☆☆☆☆☆ Admire the view from Dumpling Mountain Trail

☆☆☆☆☆ Tour the park by plane on a flightseeing tour

☆☆☆☆☆ Look for sea lions, sea otters and seals on Katmai's eastern coast

☆☆☆☆☆ Fish for salmon and rainbow trout in Brooks River

☆☆☆☆☆ Enjoy a meal at the dining room at Brooks Lodge

☆☆☆☆☆ Kayak or canoe the spectacular waters of Naknek Lake

MY PARK RATINGS:

ACTIVITIES	FEW				MANY
SCENERY	DULL				SPECTACULAR
PEOPLE	CROWDED				PEACEFUL
WILDLIFE	NONE				LOTS
OVERALL	NOT FOR ME				LOVED IT!

• •

MOST MEMORABLE MOMENTS:

• •

SPACE TO JOURNAL / DRAW / COLLECT OFFICIAL NATIONAL PARK PASSPORT STAMPS:

Kenai Fjords National Park

Est. 1980 — 669,984 acres — 59° 55' 12" N, 149° 39' 0" W

WHEN I VISITED:

WHO I WENT WITH:

WILDLIFE I SAW:

WHERE I STAYED:

FAVORITE EXPERIENCE:

WOULD I RETURN? yes/no

TOP 10 THINGS TO DO IN THIS PARK:

☆☆☆☆☆ Look for marine wildlife on a boat tour of the fjords
☆☆☆☆☆ Take a guided kayak tour of Resurrection Bay
☆☆☆☆☆ View the park's 30 glaciers from above on a flightseeing tour
☆☆☆☆☆ Hike Harding Icefield Trail across the valley floor
☆☆☆☆☆ Enjoy the view of Exit Glacier from Glacier View Loop
☆☆☆☆☆ Collect an official park stamp from the visitor center in Seward
☆☆☆☆☆ Paddleboard in Bear Lagoon's stunning glacial waters
☆☆☆☆☆ Learn about the park's glaciers at Exit Glacier Nature Center
☆☆☆☆☆ Witness a calving glacier at Holgate Glacier
☆☆☆☆☆ Hike the short but moderately strenuous Glacier Overlook Trail

MY PARK RATINGS:

ACTIVITIES	FEW				MANY
SCENERY	DULL				SPECTACULAR
PEOPLE	CROWDED				PEACEFUL
WILDLIFE	NONE				LOTS
OVERALL	NOT FOR ME				LOVED IT!

....

MOST MEMORABLE MOMENTS:

....

SPACE TO JOURNAL / DRAW / COLLECT OFFICIAL NATIONAL PARK PASSPORT STAMPS:

Kings Canyon National Park

Est. 1890 — 461,901 acres — 36° 48' 0" N, 118° 33' 0" W

WHEN I VISITED:

WHO I WENT WITH:

WILDLIFE I SAW:

WHERE I STAYED:

FAVORITE EXPERIENCE:

WOULD I RETURN? yes/no

TOP 10 THINGS TO DO IN THIS PARK:

- ☆☆☆☆☆ Drive or bike the 30-mile Kings Canyon Scenic Byway
- ☆☆☆☆☆ Walk through Fallen Monarch, a toppled sequoia's hollow base
- ☆☆☆☆☆ See the stalactites and stalagmites on a tour of Boyden Cavern
- ☆☆☆☆☆ Stand beneath General Grant, the world's 3rd largest sequoia
- ☆☆☆☆☆ Meet the endangered wild cats at Project Survival's Cat Haven
- ☆☆☆☆☆ View Redwood Canyon from the summit of Big Baldy
- ☆☆☆☆☆ Admire the view of Hume Lake from Panoramic Point Trail
- ☆☆☆☆☆ Collect an official park stamp at Kings Canyon Visitor Center
- ☆☆☆☆☆ Stroll the five-minute shaded walk to Roaring River Falls
- ☆☆☆☆☆ Hike Zumwalt Meadow Trail in the Cedar Grove area

MY PARK RATINGS:

ACTIVITIES	FEW				MANY
SCENERY	DULL				SPECTACULAR
PEOPLE	CROWDED				PEACEFUL
WILDLIFE	NONE				LOTS
OVERALL	NOT FOR ME				LOVED IT!

....

MOST MEMORABLE MOMENTS:

....

SPACE TO JOURNAL / DRAW / COLLECT OFFICIAL NATIONAL PARK PASSPORT STAMPS:

Kobuk Valley National Park

Est. 1980 — 1.8 million acres — 67° 33' 0" N, 159° 16' 48" W

WHEN I VISITED:

WHO I WENT WITH:

WILDLIFE I SAW:

WHERE I STAYED:

FAVORITE EXPERIENCE:

WOULD I RETURN? yes/no

TOP 10 THINGS TO DO IN THIS PARK:

- ☆☆☆☆☆ See Great Kobuk, the world's largest high-altitude dune field
- ☆☆☆☆☆ View the landscape from above on a flightseeing tour
- ☆☆☆☆☆ Look for wildlife along the Kobuk River
- ☆☆☆☆☆ Visit the archeological site on Paatitaaq (Onion Portage)
- ☆☆☆☆☆ Chat with a park ranger at Northwest Arctic Heritage Center
- ☆☆☆☆☆ Spend a night under the stars in the remote backcountry
- ☆☆☆☆☆ Float Kobuk or Salmon River in a kayak or collapsible canoe
- ☆☆☆☆☆ Fish for sheefish in the Pah, Black or Pick Rivers
- ☆☆☆☆☆ See a traditionally built log cabin at Giddings Cabin
- ☆☆☆☆☆ Spot a grizzly bear or black bear in the Alaskan wilderness

MY PARK RATINGS:

ACTIVITIES	FEW				MANY
SCENERY	DULL				SPECTACULAR
PEOPLE	CROWDED				PEACEFUL
WILDLIFE	NONE				LOTS
OVERALL	NOT FOR ME				LOVED IT!

....

MOST MEMORABLE MOMENTS:

....

SPACE TO JOURNAL / DRAW / COLLECT OFFICIAL NATIONAL PARK PASSPORT STAMPS:

Lake Clark National Park

Est. 1980 — 4 million acres — 60° 58' 12" N, 153° 25' 12" W

WHEN I VISITED:

WHO I WENT WITH:

WILDLIFE I SAW:

WHERE I STAYED:

FAVORITE EXPERIENCE:

WOULD I RETURN? yes/no

TOP 10 THINGS TO DO IN THIS PARK:

- ☆☆☆☆☆ Venture into the park by plane on a flightseeing tour
- ☆☆☆☆☆ Tour Dick Proenneke's cabin on Upper Twin Lake
- ☆☆☆☆☆ Explore Port Alsworth on Lake Clark's south-central shore
- ☆☆☆☆☆ Visit the indigenous Wassillie Trefon Dena'ina Fish Cache
- ☆☆☆☆☆ Hike the Tanalian Trails for views of waterfalls and lava cliffs
- ☆☆☆☆☆ Fish for salmon on Silver Salmon Creek
- ☆☆☆☆☆ Learn about the park at Port Alsworth Visitor Center
- ☆☆☆☆☆ Spend a night in one of the park's two public-use cabins
- ☆☆☆☆☆ Photograph Hnitsanghi'iy near Priest Rock Cabin
- ☆☆☆☆☆ Watch for grizzly bears along the shores of Crescent Lake

MY PARK RATINGS:

ACTIVITIES	FEW				MANY
SCENERY	DULL				SPECTACULAR
PEOPLE	CROWDED				PEACEFUL
WILDLIFE	NONE				LOTS
OVERALL	NOT FOR ME				LOVED IT!

. . . .

MOST MEMORABLE MOMENTS:

. . . .

SPACE TO JOURNAL / DRAW / COLLECT OFFICIAL NATIONAL PARK PASSPORT STAMPS:

Lassen Volcanic National Park

Est. 1916 — 106,589 acres — 40° 29' 24" N, 121° 30' 36" W

WHEN I VISITED:

WHO I WENT WITH:

WILDLIFE I SAW:

WHERE I STAYED:

FAVORITE EXPERIENCE:

WOULD I RETURN? yes/no

TOP 10 THINGS TO DO IN THIS PARK:

☆☆☆☆☆ Walk Bumpasss Hell Trail to see the hydrothermal features
☆☆☆☆☆ Kayak or canoe across picturesque Manzanita Lake
☆☆☆☆☆ Learn about the park's history at the historic Loomis Museum
☆☆☆☆☆ Hike Cascades Trail or Horse Trail to Kings Creek Falls
☆☆☆☆☆ Enjoy the 360° views of Devastated Area from Lassen Peak
☆☆☆☆☆ Drive or bike the 30-mile Lassen National Park Highway
☆☆☆☆☆ Go swimming in Juniper Lake, the park's largest lake
☆☆☆☆☆ Attend the park's Dark Sky festival for spectacular stargazing
☆☆☆☆☆ Photograph the Painted Dunes on the way to Cinder Cone
☆☆☆☆☆ Watch the park film at Kohm Yah-mah-nee Visitor Center

MY PARK RATINGS:

ACTIVITIES	FEW				MANY
SCENERY	DULL				SPECTACULAR
PEOPLE	CROWDED				PEACEFUL
WILDLIFE	NONE				LOTS
OVERALL	NOT FOR ME				LOVED IT!

....

MOST MEMORABLE MOMENTS:

....

SPACE TO JOURNAL / DRAW / COLLECT OFFICIAL NATIONAL PARK PASSPORT STAMPS:

Mammoth Cave National Park

Est. 1941 — 52,830 acres — 37° 10' 48" N, 86° 6' 0" W

WHEN I VISITED:

WHO I WENT WITH:

WILDLIFE I SAW:

WHERE I STAYED:

FAVORITE EXPERIENCE:

WOULD I RETURN? yes/no

TOP 10 THINGS TO DO IN THIS PARK:

☆☆☆☆☆ Take a ranger-led tour of Mammoth, the world's longest cave
☆☆☆☆☆ See the stalactites and stalagmites in the Frozen Niagara
☆☆☆☆☆ Take the stairs into a massive sinkhole at Cedar Sink
☆☆☆☆☆ Learn about the Cave Wars' casualty on Sand Cave Trail
☆☆☆☆☆ Traverse some of the park's above-ground trails on horseback
☆☆☆☆☆ Paddle the Green or Nolin Rivers in a kayak or canoe
☆☆☆☆☆ Explore Great Onyx Cave by lantern on a guided tour
☆☆☆☆☆ Ride the Green River Ferry, one of the country's oldest ferries
☆☆☆☆☆ Journey along Mammoth Cave Railroad Hike & Bike Trail
☆☆☆☆☆ Locate the grave of Stephen Bishop at Old Guide's Cemetery

MY PARK RATINGS:

ACTIVITIES	FEW				MANY
SCENERY	DULL				SPECTACULAR
PEOPLE	CROWDED				PEACEFUL
WILDLIFE	NONE				LOTS
OVERALL	NOT FOR ME				LOVED IT!

··

MOST MEMORABLE MOMENTS:

··

SPACE TO JOURNAL / DRAW / COLLECT OFFICIAL NATIONAL PARK PASSPORT STAMPS:

Mesa Verde National Park

Est. 1906 — 52,485 acres — 37° 10' 48" N, 108° 29' 24" W

WHEN I VISITED:

WHO I WENT WITH:

WILDLIFE I SAW:

WHERE I STAYED:

FAVORITE EXPERIENCE:

WOULD I RETURN? yes/no

TOP 10 THINGS TO DO IN THIS PARK:

- ☆☆☆☆☆ Visit Cliff Palace, Balcony House or Long House on a tour
- ☆☆☆☆☆ Take a self-guided tour of the Step House cliff dwelling
- ☆☆☆☆☆ View the Spruce Tree House from Spruce Tree Overlook
- ☆☆☆☆☆ See the Spruce and Navajo canyons on Petroglyph Point Trail
- ☆☆☆☆☆ Explore Chapin Mesa Archeological Museum
- ☆☆☆☆☆ Drive or bike the scenic 6-mile Mesa Top Loop road
- ☆☆☆☆☆ Learn about Puebloan life at the Far View Sites
- ☆☆☆☆☆ Enjoy the view from Park Point Fire Lookout
- ☆☆☆☆☆ Peek inside the ancient windows of Sun Temple
- ☆☆☆☆☆ Observe Square Tower House, the park's tallest cliff dwelling

MY PARK RATINGS:

ACTIVITIES	FEW				MANY
SCENERY	DULL				SPECTACULAR
PEOPLE	CROWDED				PEACEFUL
WILDLIFE	NONE				LOTS
OVERALL	NOT FOR ME				LOVED IT!

....

MOST MEMORABLE MOMENTS:

....

SPACE TO JOURNAL / DRAW / COLLECT OFFICIAL NATIONAL PARK PASSPORT STAMPS:

Mount Rainier National Park

Est. 1899 — 236,381 acres — 46° 51' 0" N, 121° 45' 0" W

WHEN I VISITED:

WHO I WENT WITH:

WILDLIFE I SAW:

WHERE I STAYED:

FAVORITE EXPERIENCE:

WOULD I RETURN? yes/no

TOP 10 THINGS TO DO IN THIS PARK:

- ☆☆☆☆☆ View the park's alpine ridges and meadows from Skyline Trail
- ☆☆☆☆☆ Ride the gondola to the peak of Crystal Mountain
- ☆☆☆☆☆ Adventure into the wilderness on the famed Wonderland Trail
- ☆☆☆☆☆ Look out over Paradise from Panorama Point
- ☆☆☆☆☆ Feel the spray of the waterfall at Narada Falls
- ☆☆☆☆☆ Enjoy a five-star brunch at the historic Paradise Inn
- ☆☆☆☆☆ Photograph Mount Rainier from the shores of Reflection Lake
- ☆☆☆☆☆ Stand among 1,000-year-old trees in Grove of the Patriarchs
- ☆☆☆☆☆ Relax in front of the fireplace at the historic National Park Inn
- ☆☆☆☆☆ Look for wildlife along Sourdough Ridge Nature Trail

MY PARK RATINGS:

ACTIVITIES	FEW				MANY
SCENERY	DULL				SPECTACULAR
PEOPLE	CROWDED				PEACEFUL
WILDLIFE	NONE				LOTS
OVERALL	NOT FOR ME				LOVED IT!

....

MOST MEMORABLE MOMENTS:

....

SPACE TO JOURNAL / DRAW / COLLECT OFFICIAL NATIONAL PARK PASSPORT STAMPS:

NP of American Samoa

Est. 1899 — 236,381 acres — 46° 51' 0" N, 121° 45' 0" W

WHEN I VISITED:

WHO I WENT WITH:

WILDLIFE I SAW:

WHERE I STAYED:

FAVORITE EXPERIENCE:

WOULD I RETURN? yes/no

TOP 10 THINGS TO DO IN THIS PARK:

☆ ☆ ☆ ☆ ☆ Wade into the warm waters of the Pacific at Ofu Beach
☆ ☆ ☆ ☆ ☆ Snorkel in the National Marine Sanctuary of American Samoa
☆ ☆ ☆ ☆ ☆ See Samoa's oldest settlement on Si'u Point Trail
☆ ☆ ☆ ☆ ☆ Spot a fruit bat while hiking Mount 'Alava Trail
☆ ☆ ☆ ☆ ☆ Immerse yourself in Samoan culture during a homestay
☆ ☆ ☆ ☆ ☆ View the Vai'ava Strait from Lower Sauma Ridge Trail
☆ ☆ ☆ ☆ ☆ See all seven of Samoa's National Natural Landmarks
☆ ☆ ☆ ☆ ☆ Take a stroll on Oge Beach and look for boobies
☆ ☆ ☆ ☆ ☆ Learn about Samoan culture at the Jean P. Haydon Museum
☆ ☆ ☆ ☆ ☆ Collect an official park passport stamp from the visitor center

MY PARK RATINGS:

ACTIVITIES	FEW				MANY
SCENERY	DULL				SPECTACULAR
PEOPLE	CROWDED				PEACEFUL
WILDLIFE	NONE				LOTS
OVERALL	NOT FOR ME				LOVED IT!

· ·

MOST MEMORABLE MOMENTS:

· ·

SPACE TO JOURNAL / DRAW / COLLECT OFFICIAL NATIONAL PARK PASSPORT STAMPS:

New River Gorge National Park

Est. 2021 — 70,000 acres — 37° 55' 36" N, 81° 9' 18" W

WHEN I VISITED:

WHO I WENT WITH:

WILDLIFE I SAW:

WHERE I STAYED:

FAVORITE EXPERIENCE:

WOULD I RETURN? yes/no

TOP 10 THINGS TO DO IN THIS PARK:

- ☆☆☆☆☆ Take a guided tour along the length of New River Gorge Bridge
- ☆☆☆☆☆ Admire the view from Diamond Point on Endless Wall Trail
- ☆☆☆☆☆ Visit the historic Kaymoor One Mining Complex
- ☆☆☆☆☆ Hike or mountain bike Long Point Trail
- ☆☆☆☆☆ Drive or bike the 83-mile New River Gorge Scenic Drive
- ☆☆☆☆☆ Go white-water rafting on the New River
- ☆☆☆☆☆ Take a walking tour of historic Thurmond
- ☆☆☆☆☆ View Wolf Creek from the Fayetteville Trail trailhead
- ☆☆☆☆☆ See New River's horseshoe bend from Grandview Overlook
- ☆☆☆☆☆ Visit Sandstone Falls, the park's largest waterfall

MY PARK RATINGS:

ACTIVITIES	FEW				MANY
SCENERY	DULL				SPECTACULAR
PEOPLE	CROWDED				PEACEFUL
WILDLIFE	NONE				LOTS
OVERALL	NOT FOR ME				LOVED IT!

....

MOST MEMORABLE MOMENTS:

....

SPACE TO JOURNAL / DRAW / COLLECT OFFICIAL NATIONAL PARK PASSPORT STAMPS:

North Cascades National Park

Est. 1968 — 504,781 acres — 48° 42' 0" N, 121° 12' 0" W

WHEN I VISITED:

WHO I WENT WITH:

WILDLIFE I SAW:

WHERE I STAYED:

FAVORITE EXPERIENCE:

WOULD I RETURN? yes/no

TOP 10 THINGS TO DO IN THIS PARK:

- ☆☆☆☆☆ Drive or bike the scenic 30-mile North Cascades Highway
- ☆☆☆☆☆ See Diablo Lake from the Diablo Lake Vista Point
- ☆☆☆☆☆ Admire the panoramic views along Maple Pass Loop
- ☆☆☆☆☆ Look for wildlife along Rainy Lake Trail
- ☆☆☆☆☆ View the Skagit Gorge and dam from Gorge Lake Overlook
- ☆☆☆☆☆ See the park as author Jack Kerouac did from Desolation Peak
- ☆☆☆☆☆ Learn about local culture while exploring the village of Stehekin
- ☆☆☆☆☆ Dip your toes in the freezing waters of Blue Lake
- ☆☆☆☆☆ Stand on top of a glacier on Sahale Glacier Trail
- ☆☆☆☆☆ Pick apples from the orchard at the Buckner Homestead

MY PARK RATINGS:

ACTIVITIES	FEW				MANY
SCENERY	DULL				SPECTACULAR
PEOPLE	CROWDED				PEACEFUL
WILDLIFE	NONE				LOTS
OVERALL	NOT FOR ME				LOVED IT!

....

MOST MEMORABLE MOMENTS:

....

SPACE TO JOURNAL / DRAW / COLLECT OFFICIAL NATIONAL PARK PASSPORT STAMPS:

Olympic National Park

WA — Est. 1938 — 922,650 acres — 47° 58' 12" N, 123° 30' 0" W

WHEN I VISITED:

WHO I WENT WITH:

WILDLIFE I SAW:

WHERE I STAYED:

FAVORITE EXPERIENCE:

WOULD I RETURN? yes/no

TOP 10 THINGS TO DO IN THIS PARK:

☆☆☆☆☆ View the Olympic mountain range from Hurricane Ridge
☆☆☆☆☆ Look for sea otters and bald eagles at Ruby Beach
☆☆☆☆☆ Explore the Hoh Rain Forest on Hoh River Trail
☆☆☆☆☆ See the thundering Sol Duc Falls on Sol Duc River Trail
☆☆☆☆☆ Explore the glacial Lake Crescent by kayak or canoe
☆☆☆☆☆ View Lake Crescent from the peak of Mt. Storm King
☆☆☆☆☆ Take a stroll through giant spruce trees to Marymere Falls
☆☆☆☆☆ Visit Cape Flattery, the contiguous U.S.'s northernmost point
☆☆☆☆☆ Look for marine life in the tidepools at Shi Shi Beach
☆☆☆☆☆ Walk the rocky coastline of Rialto Beach to Hole in the Wall

MY PARK RATINGS:

ACTIVITIES	FEW				MANY
SCENERY	DULL				SPECTACULAR
PEOPLE	CROWDED				PEACEFUL
WILDLIFE	NONE				LOTS
OVERALL	NOT FOR ME				LOVED IT!

··

MOST MEMORABLE MOMENTS:

··

SPACE TO JOURNAL / DRAW / COLLECT OFFICIAL NATIONAL PARK PASSPORT STAMPS:

Petrified Forest National Park

AZ — Est. 1962 — 221,416 acres — 35° 4' 12" N, 109° 46' 48" W

WHEN I VISITED:

WHO I WENT WITH:

WILDLIFE I SAW:

WHERE I STAYED:

FAVORITE EXPERIENCE:

WOULD I RETURN? yes/no

TOP 10 THINGS TO DO IN THIS PARK:

- ☆☆☆☆☆ Drive or bike the 28-mile Painted Desert Scenic Drive
- ☆☆☆☆☆ Photograph Old Faithful on Giant Logs Interpretive Loop Trail
- ☆☆☆☆☆ See the petroglyphs at Newspaper Rock or Puerco Pueblo
- ☆☆☆☆☆ View the cultural exhibits at Painted Desert Inn
- ☆☆☆☆☆ Explore the 700-year-old Agate House, an eight-room pueblo
- ☆☆☆☆☆ See traces of the original roadbed of historic Route 66
- ☆☆☆☆☆ Drive Petrified Forest Road through the colorful Tepees
- ☆☆☆☆☆ Stroll through the banded hills of Blue Mesa on Blue Mesa Trail
- ☆☆☆☆☆ See the vast array of petrified wood at Jasper Forest Overlook
- ☆☆☆☆☆ Chat with a park ranger at Painted Desert Visitor Center

MY PARK RATINGS:

ACTIVITIES	FEW				MANY
SCENERY	DULL				SPECTACULAR
PEOPLE	CROWDED				PEACEFUL
WILDLIFE	NONE				LOTS
OVERALL	NOT FOR ME				LOVED IT!

....

MOST MEMORABLE MOMENTS:

....

SPACE TO JOURNAL / DRAW / COLLECT OFFICIAL NATIONAL PARK PASSPORT STAMPS:

Pinnacles National Park

Est. 2013 — 26,686 acres — 36° 28' 48" N, 121° 9' 36" W

WHEN I VISITED:

WHO I WENT WITH:

WILDLIFE I SAW:

WHERE I STAYED:

FAVORITE EXPERIENCE:

WOULD I RETURN? yes/no

TOP 10 THINGS TO DO IN THIS PARK:

- ☆☆☆☆☆ Explore the Bear Gulch cave system by flashlight
- ☆☆☆☆☆ Take in the view of the High Peaks from Condor Gulch Trail
- ☆☆☆☆☆ Visit the historic Bacon and Butterfield Homesteads
- ☆☆☆☆☆ Watch a film about the park at the Bear Gulch Nature Center
- ☆☆☆☆☆ Look for condors at the Peaks View scenic overlook
- ☆☆☆☆☆ Hike Juniper Canyon Loop through the heart of the High Peaks
- ☆☆☆☆☆ Explore the Balconies cave system by flashlight
- ☆☆☆☆☆ See the High Peaks and Hain Wilderness from Prewett Point
- ☆☆☆☆☆ Admire the park's dark skies while stargazing with a ranger
- ☆☆☆☆☆ Collect an official park stamp at Pinnacles Visitor Center

MY PARK RATINGS:

ACTIVITIES	FEW				MANY
SCENERY	DULL				SPECTACULAR
PEOPLE	CROWDED				PEACEFUL
WILDLIFE	NONE				LOTS
OVERALL	NOT FOR ME				LOVED IT!

. . . .

MOST MEMORABLE MOMENTS:

. . . .

SPACE TO JOURNAL / DRAW / COLLECT OFFICIAL NATIONAL PARK PASSPORT STAMPS:

Redwood National Park

Est. 1968 — 138,999 acres — 41° 18' 0" N, 124° 0' 0" W

WHEN I VISITED:

WHO I WENT WITH:

WILDLIFE I SAW:

WHERE I STAYED:

FAVORITE EXPERIENCE:

WOULD I RETURN? yes/no

TOP 10 THINGS TO DO IN THIS PARK:

☆☆☆☆☆ Take a peaceful stroll through Lady Bird Johnson Grove
☆☆☆☆☆ See where the river meets the sea at Klamath River Overlook
☆☆☆☆☆ Wander through the redwoods in search of Trillium Falls
☆☆☆☆☆ Explore the tidepools with a park ranger at Enderts Beach
☆☆☆☆☆ Swim in the coastal waters at Gold Bluffs Beach
☆☆☆☆☆ Explore sections of the stunning 70-mile Coastal Trail
☆☆☆☆☆ Photograph the Roosevelt elk at Elk Prairie
☆☆☆☆☆ Visit the Big Tree on Cathedral Tree Trail Loop
☆☆☆☆☆ See the place where Jurassic Park 2 filmed in Fern Canyon
☆☆☆☆☆ Watch for whales at Thomas H. Kuchel Visitor Center

MY PARK RATINGS:

ACTIVITIES	FEW				MANY
SCENERY	DULL				SPECTACULAR
PEOPLE	CROWDED				PEACEFUL
WILDLIFE	NONE				LOTS
OVERALL	NOT FOR ME				LOVED IT!

• •

MOST MEMORABLE MOMENTS:

• •

SPACE TO JOURNAL / DRAW / COLLECT OFFICIAL NATIONAL PARK PASSPORT STAMPS:

Rocky Mountain National Park

CO

Est. 1915 — 265,795 acres — 40° 24' 0" N, 105° 34' 48" W

WHEN I VISITED:

WHO I WENT WITH:

WILDLIFE I SAW:

WHERE I STAYED:

FAVORITE EXPERIENCE:

WOULD I RETURN? yes/no

TOP 10 THINGS TO DO IN THIS PARK:

☆☆☆☆☆ Drive or bike the 48-mile Trail Ridge Road
☆☆☆☆☆ Admire the panoramic view from Forest Canyon Overlook
☆☆☆☆☆ Look for elk along Alpine Ridge Trail
☆☆☆☆☆ Take the park shuttle for a ride along 23-mile Bear Lake Road
☆☆☆☆☆ Hike Glacier Gorge Trail to the park's famed Alberta Falls
☆☆☆☆☆ Overlook Moraine Park from the summit of Deer Mountain
☆☆☆☆☆ Tour the hundred-year-old property at Holzwarth Historic Site
☆☆☆☆☆ Drive or mountain bike Old Fall River Road to Chasm Falls
☆☆☆☆☆ Photograph the Continental Divide from Milner Pass
☆☆☆☆☆ See all three breathtaking waterfalls on Bluebird Lake Trail

MY PARK RATINGS:

ACTIVITIES	FEW				MANY
SCENERY	DULL				SPECTACULAR
PEOPLE	CROWDED				PEACEFUL
WILDLIFE	NONE				LOTS
OVERALL	NOT FOR ME				LOVED IT!

....

MOST MEMORABLE MOMENTS:

....

SPACE TO JOURNAL / DRAW / COLLECT OFFICIAL
NATIONAL PARK PASSPORT STAMPS:

Saguaro National Park

AZ

Est. 1994 — 91,442 acres — 32° 15' 0" N, 110° 30' 0" W

WHEN I VISITED:

WHO I WENT WITH:

WILDLIFE I SAW:

WHERE I STAYED:

FAVORITE EXPERIENCE:

WOULD I RETURN? yes/no

TOP 10 THINGS TO DO IN THIS PARK:

- ☆☆☆☆☆ Drive or bike the 6-mile Bajada Loop in Saguaro West
- ☆☆☆☆☆ See the Saguaro cacti up close on Valley View Overlook Trail
- ☆☆☆☆☆ View the 800-year-old Hohokam petroglyphs at Signal Hill
- ☆☆☆☆☆ Learn about the park on Desert Discovery Nature Trail
- ☆☆☆☆☆ Admire the park from the top of Wasson Peak
- ☆☆☆☆☆ Drive or bike the 8-mile Cactus Forest Drive in Saguaro East
- ☆☆☆☆☆ Look for roadrunners and other wildlife along Mica View Trail
- ☆☆☆☆☆ Hike or mountain bike Hope Camp Trail through Rincon Valley
- ☆☆☆☆☆ Take a self-guided nature walk along Cactus Garden Trail
- ☆☆☆☆☆ Collect an official park stamp from Red Hills Visitor Center

MY PARK RATINGS:

ACTIVITIES	FEW				MANY
SCENERY	DULL				SPECTACULAR
PEOPLE	CROWDED				PEACEFUL
WILDLIFE	NONE				LOTS
OVERALL	NOT FOR ME				LOVED IT!

··

MOST MEMORABLE MOMENTS:

··

SPACE TO JOURNAL / DRAW / COLLECT OFFICIAL NATIONAL PARK PASSPORT STAMPS:

Sequoia National Park

Est. 1890 — 404,063 acres — 36° 25' 48" N, 118° 40' 48" W

WHEN I VISITED:

WHO I WENT WITH:

WILDLIFE I SAW:

WHERE I STAYED:

FAVORITE EXPERIENCE:

WOULD I RETURN? yes/no

TOP 10 THINGS TO DO IN THIS PARK:

☆☆☆☆☆ Stand beneath General Sherman, the world's largest tree
☆☆☆☆☆ Walk among giant sequoias on Congress Trail
☆☆☆☆☆ Climb the steps to the granite peak of Moro Rock
☆☆☆☆☆ Learn about the park's giant trees at Giant Forest Museum
☆☆☆☆☆ Drive Generals Highway between Sequoia and Kings Canyon
☆☆☆☆☆ Tour Crystal Cave's marble and limestone formations
☆☆☆☆☆ Drive Crescent Meadow Road through the famed Tunnel Log
☆☆☆☆☆ Admire the wildflowers in Crescent Meadow
☆☆☆☆☆ Watch the park film at Lodgepole Visitor Center
☆☆☆☆☆ See the indigenous pictographs on Hospital Rock

MY PARK RATINGS:

ACTIVITIES	FEW				MANY
SCENERY	DULL				SPECTACULAR
PEOPLE	CROWDED				PEACEFUL
WILDLIFE	NONE				LOTS
OVERALL	NOT FOR ME				LOVED IT!

....

MOST MEMORABLE MOMENTS:

....

SPACE TO JOURNAL / DRAW / COLLECT OFFICIAL NATIONAL PARK PASSPORT STAMPS:

Shenandoah National Park

Est. 1935 — 199,117 acres — 38° 31' 48" N, 78° 21' 0" W

WHEN I VISITED:

WHO I WENT WITH:

WILDLIFE I SAW:

WHERE I STAYED:

☺ ☺ ☹

FAVORITE EXPERIENCE:

WOULD I RETURN? yes/no

TOP 10 THINGS TO DO IN THIS PARK:

☆☆☆☆☆ Drive or bike the scenic 105-mile Skyline Drive
☆☆☆☆☆ Enjoy 360° views of the park after a hike to the top of Old Rag
☆☆☆☆☆ Take a ranger-led tour of historic retreat Rapidan Camp
☆☆☆☆☆ Photograph the landscape from Range View Overlook
☆☆☆☆☆ Scramble up boulders to the summit of Bearfence Mountain
☆☆☆☆☆ Hike the park's two tallest peaks: Hawksbill and Stony Man
☆☆☆☆☆ Admire the Shenandoah Valley from Blackrock Summit
☆☆☆☆☆ Imagine what early 20th century life was like at Snead Farm
☆☆☆☆☆ Chat with a park ranger at Dickey Ridge Visitor Center
☆☆☆☆☆ Hike a portion of the famed Appalachian Trail

MY PARK RATINGS:

ACTIVITIES	FEW				MANY
SCENERY	DULL				SPECTACULAR
PEOPLE	CROWDED				PEACEFUL
WILDLIFE	NONE				LOTS
OVERALL	NOT FOR ME				LOVED IT!

....

MOST MEMORABLE MOMENTS:

....

SPACE TO JOURNAL / DRAW / COLLECT OFFICIAL NATIONAL PARK PASSPORT STAMPS:

Theodore Roosevelt NP

ND

Est. 1935 — 199,117 acres — 38° 31' 48" N, 78° 21' 0" W

WHEN I VISITED:

WHO I WENT WITH:

WILDLIFE I SAW:

WHERE I STAYED:

FAVORITE EXPERIENCE:

WOULD I RETURN? yes/no

TOP 10 THINGS TO DO IN THIS PARK:

☆☆☆☆☆ Admire the stunning 360° badlands views from Buck Hill
☆☆☆☆☆ Visit Theodore Roosevelt's historic Maltese Cross Ranch Cabin
☆☆☆☆☆ Drive or bike the 14-mile North Unit Scenic Drive
☆☆☆☆☆ Observe the prairie dog towns on Buckhorn Trail
☆☆☆☆☆ Hike part of the 144-mile Maah Daah Hey Trail
☆☆☆☆☆ View the Little Missouri River from Little Mo Nature Trail
☆☆☆☆☆ Drive or bike the 24-mile South Unit Scenic Drive
☆☆☆☆☆ Admire the bluish-gray hills from Bentonitic Clay Viewpoint
☆☆☆☆☆ See bison, coyotes, mule deer and more at Oxbox Overlook
☆☆☆☆☆ Dip your toes in the Little Missouri River in the South Unit

MY PARK RATINGS:

ACTIVITIES	FEW				MANY
SCENERY	DULL				SPECTACULAR
PEOPLE	CROWDED				PEACEFUL
WILDLIFE	NONE				LOTS
OVERALL	NOT FOR ME				LOVED IT!

．．．

MOST MEMORABLE MOMENTS:

．．．

SPACE TO JOURNAL / DRAW / COLLECT OFFICIAL NATIONAL PARK PASSPORT STAMPS:

Virgin Islands National Park

Est. 1956 — 14,948 acres — 18° 19' 48" N, 64° 43' 48" W

WHEN I VISITED:

WHO I WENT WITH:

WILDLIFE I SAW:

WHERE I STAYED:

FAVORITE EXPERIENCE:

WOULD I RETURN? yes/no

TOP 10 THINGS TO DO IN THIS PARK:

☆☆☆☆☆ Lounge beneath leaning palm trees on the beachs of Trunk Bay
☆☆☆☆☆ See the petroglyphs while hiking Reef Bay Trail
☆☆☆☆☆ Rent a kayak or paddleboard at Honeymoon Beach
☆☆☆☆☆ Take a walk on the rocky beach of Salt Pond Bay
☆☆☆☆☆ Admire the 360° view of Saint John from Ram Head Trail
☆☆☆☆☆ Snorkel with sea turtles in the warm waters of Maho Bay
☆☆☆☆☆ Hike the Cinnamon Bay Nature Trail to the America Hill Ruins
☆☆☆☆☆ Explore the ruins of Reef Bay Sugar Factory
☆☆☆☆☆ Walk Peace Hill Trail at sunset to secluded Denis Bay
☆☆☆☆☆ Kayak to Whistling Cay and take a self-guided tour of the ruins

MY PARK RATINGS:

ACTIVITIES	FEW				MANY
SCENERY	DULL				SPECTACULAR
PEOPLE	CROWDED				PEACEFUL
WILDLIFE	NONE				LOTS
OVERALL	NOT FOR ME				LOVED IT!

....

MOST MEMORABLE MOMENTS:

....

SPACE TO JOURNAL / DRAW / COLLECT OFFICIAL
NATIONAL PARK PASSPORT STAMPS:

Voyageurs National Park

Est. 1975 — 218,200 acres — 48° 30' 0" N, 92° 52' 48" W

WHEN I VISITED:

WHO I WENT WITH:

WILDLIFE I SAW:

WHERE I STAYED:

FAVORITE EXPERIENCE:

WOULD I RETURN? yes/no

TOP 10 THINGS TO DO IN THIS PARK:

- ☆☆☆☆☆ Explore Rainy Lake on the ranger-led Voyageur tour boat
- ☆☆☆☆☆ Admire the terraced flower beds at Ellsworth Rock Gardens
- ☆☆☆☆☆ Hike Cruiser Lake Trail from Kabetogama Lake to Rainy Lake
- ☆☆☆☆☆ Collect an official park stamp at Rainy Lake Visitor Center
- ☆☆☆☆☆ Imagine life as a voyageur on a guided canoe tour of Rainy Lake
- ☆☆☆☆☆ Spend the night in a houseboat on Namakan Lake
- ☆☆☆☆☆ Fish for walleye on the 25,000-acre Kabetogama Lake
- ☆☆☆☆☆ Visit the Kettle Falls Hotel's famous bar and its tilted floor
- ☆☆☆☆☆ Stand on the Canadian shore of Sand Point Lake
- ☆☆☆☆☆ Admire the view from both overlooks on Oberholtzer Trail

MY PARK RATINGS:

ACTIVITIES	FEW				MANY
SCENERY	DULL				SPECTACULAR
PEOPLE	CROWDED				PEACEFUL
WILDLIFE	NONE				LOTS
OVERALL	NOT FOR ME				LOVED IT!

....

MOST MEMORABLE MOMENTS:

....

SPACE TO JOURNAL / DRAW / COLLECT OFFICIAL
NATIONAL PARK PASSPORT STAMPS:

White Sands National Park

NM — Est. 2019 — 176,000 acres — 32° 46' 47" N, 106° 10' 18" W

WHEN I VISITED:

WHO I WENT WITH:

WILDLIFE I SAW:

WHERE I STAYED:

FAVORITE EXPERIENCE:

WOULD I RETURN? yes/no

TOP 10 THINGS TO DO IN THIS PARK:

- ☆☆☆☆☆ Drive or bike the scenic 8-mile Dunes Drive
- ☆☆☆☆☆ See Chihuahuan Desert plant life at the Native Plant Garden
- ☆☆☆☆☆ Hike the otherworldly Alkali Flat Trail across an ancient lakebed
- ☆☆☆☆☆ Learn about the park's geology on the Interdune Boardwalk
- ☆☆☆☆☆ Look for desert wildlife along Dune Life Nature Trail
- ☆☆☆☆☆ Explore the exhibits at White Sands Visitor Center
- ☆☆☆☆☆ Admire the park's dark skies on a ranger-led full moon hike
- ☆☆☆☆☆ Go sledding in the sand dunes near Interdune Boardwalk
- ☆☆☆☆☆ Learn about the park's geology on a ranger-led sunset stroll
- ☆☆☆☆☆ Enjoy a picnic at the Primrose or Roadrunner picnic areas

MY PARK RATINGS:

ACTIVITIES	FEW				MANY
SCENERY	DULL				SPECTACULAR
PEOPLE	CROWDED				PEACEFUL
WILDLIFE	NONE				LOTS
OVERALL	NOT FOR ME				LOVED IT!

....

MOST MEMORABLE MOMENTS:

....

SPACE TO JOURNAL / DRAW / COLLECT OFFICIAL NATIONAL PARK PASSPORT STAMPS:

Wind Cave National Park

SD — Est. 1903 — 33,924 acres — 43° 34' 12" N, 103° 28' 48" W

WHEN I VISITED:

WHO I WENT WITH:

WILDLIFE I SAW:

WHERE I STAYED:

FAVORITE EXPERIENCE:

WOULD I RETURN? yes/no

TOP 10 THINGS TO DO IN THIS PARK:

- ☆☆☆☆☆ Admire Wind Cave's unique boxwork formations
- ☆☆☆☆☆ Explore one of the world's longest caves on a ranger-led tour
- ☆☆☆☆☆ See the vast South Dakota prairie from Rankin Ridge Trail
- ☆☆☆☆☆ Look for bison, prairie dogs and pronghorn at Bison Flats
- ☆☆☆☆☆ Take a leisurely stroll through the grassland on Prairie Vista Trail
- ☆☆☆☆☆ Drive or bike the park's breathtaking dirt backroads: NPS 5 & 6
- ☆☆☆☆☆ Birdwatch for cliff swallows and owls in Wind Cave Canyon
- ☆☆☆☆☆ Collect an official park stamp at Wind Cave Visitor Center
- ☆☆☆☆☆ Enjoy the panoramic views from Boland Ridge Trail
- ☆☆☆☆☆ Drive or bike Bison Flats Drive or Rankin Ridge Drive

MY PARK RATINGS:

ACTIVITIES	FEW				MANY
SCENERY	DULL				SPECTACULAR
PEOPLE	CROWDED				PEACEFUL
WILDLIFE	NONE				LOTS
OVERALL	NOT FOR ME				LOVED IT!

....

MOST MEMORABLE MOMENTS:

....

SPACE TO JOURNAL / DRAW / COLLECT OFFICIAL NATIONAL PARK PASSPORT STAMPS:

Wrangell-St. Elias National Park

Est. 1980 — 13.1 million acres — 61° 0' 0" N, 142° 0' 0" W

WHEN I VISITED:

WHO I WENT WITH:

WILDLIFE I SAW:

WHERE I STAYED:

FAVORITE EXPERIENCE:

WOULD I RETURN? yes/no

TOP 10 THINGS TO DO IN THIS PARK:

- ☆☆☆☆☆ Drive or bike the bumpy 60-mile McCarthy Road
- ☆☆☆☆☆ Learn about indigenous culture at the Ahtna Cultural Center
- ☆☆☆☆☆ Cross Kuskulana River Canyon on the single-lane bridge
- ☆☆☆☆☆ Explore the historic mining towns of McCarthy and Kennecott
- ☆☆☆☆☆ Drive into the northern foothills on 45-mile Nabesna Road
- ☆☆☆☆☆ View the Copper River from Copper River Bluff Trail
- ☆☆☆☆☆ Visit the Kennecott Mines National Historic Landmark
- ☆☆☆☆☆ Admire the park's more remote areas on a flightseeing tour
- ☆☆☆☆☆ Stand on top of a glacier on Root Glacier Trail
- ☆☆☆☆☆ Chat with a ranger at Copper Center Complex Visitor Center

MY PARK RATINGS:

ACTIVITIES	FEW				MANY
SCENERY	DULL				SPECTACULAR
PEOPLE	CROWDED				PEACEFUL
WILDLIFE	NONE				LOTS
OVERALL	NOT FOR ME				LOVED IT!

....

MOST MEMORABLE MOMENTS:

....

SPACE TO JOURNAL / DRAW / COLLECT OFFICIAL NATIONAL PARK PASSPORT STAMPS:

Yellowstone National Park

WY

Est. 1872 — 2.2 million acres — 44° 36' 0" N, 110° 30' 0" W

WHEN I VISITED:

WHO I WENT WITH:

WILDLIFE I SAW:

WHERE I STAYED:

FAVORITE EXPERIENCE:

WOULD I RETURN? yes/no

TOP 10 THINGS TO DO IN THIS PARK:

☆☆☆☆☆ Witness the famous eruption of Old Faithful
☆☆☆☆☆ Peer into Morning Glory Pool in Upper Geyser Basin
☆☆☆☆☆ Take a stroll on the boardwalk along the Grand Prismatic Spring
☆☆☆☆☆ Hike through the lodgepole forest to Fairy Falls
☆☆☆☆☆ See the Grand Canyon of the Yellowstone from the South Rim
☆☆☆☆☆ Observe the park's iconic bison herds in Lamar Valley
☆☆☆☆☆ Drive or bike the 19-mile Dunraven Pass
☆☆☆☆☆ Enjoy panoramic views from the peak of Mt. Washburn
☆☆☆☆☆ Visit the travertine terraces of Mammoth Hot Springs
☆☆☆☆☆ Swim in the Boiling River Hot Springs in Gardner River

MY PARK RATINGS:

ACTIVITIES	FEW				MANY
SCENERY	DULL				SPECTACULAR
PEOPLE	CROWDED				PEACEFUL
WILDLIFE	NONE				LOTS
OVERALL	NOT FOR ME				LOVED IT!

· ·

MOST MEMORABLE MOMENTS:

· ·

SPACE TO JOURNAL / DRAW / COLLECT OFFICIAL NATIONAL PARK PASSPORT STAMPS:

Yosemite National Park

Est. 1890 — 761,348 acres — 37° 49' 48" N, 119° 30' 0" W

WHEN I VISITED:

WHO I WENT WITH:

WILDLIFE I SAW:

WHERE I STAYED:

FAVORITE EXPERIENCE:

WOULD I RETURN? yes/no

TOP 10 THINGS TO DO IN THIS PARK:

- ☆☆☆☆☆ Drive or bike the scenic 59-mile Tioga Road
- ☆☆☆☆☆ See Half Dome from Sentinel Bridge at sunset
- ☆☆☆☆☆ Stand beneath Grizzly Giant in the Mariposa Grove
- ☆☆☆☆☆ Visit Yosemite Falls, North America's highest waterfall
- ☆☆☆☆☆ Learn about the park's indigenous history at Yosemite Musem
- ☆☆☆☆☆ Explore the glacier-carved valley of Hetch Hetchy
- ☆☆☆☆☆ Enjoy a delicious meal at The Ahwahnee Dining Room
- ☆☆☆☆☆ Go horseback riding through wildflowers in Wawona Meadow
- ☆☆☆☆☆ Take one of the Yosemite Nature Conservancy's many classes
- ☆☆☆☆☆ Watch Horsetail Fall rush over the edge of El Capitan

MY PARK RATINGS:

ACTIVITIES	FEW				MANY
SCENERY	DULL				SPECTACULAR
PEOPLE	CROWDED				PEACEFUL
WILDLIFE	NONE				LOTS
OVERALL	NOT FOR ME				LOVED IT!

....

MOST MEMORABLE MOMENTS:

....

SPACE TO JOURNAL / DRAW / COLLECT OFFICIAL NATIONAL PARK PASSPORT STAMPS:

Zion National Park
UT
Est. 1919 — 147,237 acres — 37° 18' 0" N, 113° 3' 0" W

WHEN I VISITED:

WHO I WENT WITH:

WILDLIFE I SAW:

WHERE I STAYED:

FAVORITE EXPERIENCE:

WOULD I RETURN? yes/no

TOP 10 THINGS TO DO IN THIS PARK:

☆☆☆☆☆ Hike the Virgin River through the famed Narrows

☆☆☆☆☆ Watch the sunset from Canyon Junction Bridge

☆☆☆☆☆ Hike Angels Landing Trail or Canyon Overlook Trail

☆☆☆☆☆ Observe the multiple waterfalls at Emerald Pools

☆☆☆☆☆ Drive or bike the 5-mile Kolob Canyons Road

☆☆☆☆☆ Ride the park shuttle along Zion Canyon Scenic Drive

☆☆☆☆☆ Drive or bike the Zion-Mount Carmel Highway and Tunnels

☆☆☆☆☆ Learn about local inhabitants at Zion Human History Museum

☆☆☆☆☆ Look out over Zion Canyon from Canyon Overlook

☆☆☆☆☆ Admire the unbelievable view from Observation Point

MY PARK RATINGS:

ACTIVITIES	FEW				MANY
SCENERY	DULL				SPECTACULAR
PEOPLE	CROWDED				PEACEFUL
WILDLIFE	NONE				LOTS
OVERALL	NOT FOR ME				LOVED IT!

....

MOST MEMORABLE MOMENTS:

....

SPACE TO JOURNAL / DRAW / COLLECT OFFICIAL
NATIONAL PARK PASSPORT STAMPS:

BUCKET LIST:

1.

Date:
National Park:

2.

Date:
National Park:

3.

Date:
National Park:

4.

Date:
National Park:

5.

Date:
National Park:

6.

Date:
National Park:

7.

Date:
National Park:

8.

Date:
National Park:

9.

Date:
National Park:

10.

Date:
National Park:

COMPLETED ON:

BUCKET LIST:

1.

Date:
National Park:

2.

Date:
National Park:

3.

Date:
National Park:

4.

Date:
National Park:

5.

Date:
National Park:

6.

Date:
National Park:

7.

Date:
National Park:

8.

Date:
National Park:

9.

Date:
National Park:

10.

Date:
National Park:

COMPLETED ON:

BUCKET LIST:

1.

Date:
National Park:

2.

Date:
National Park:

3.

Date:
National Park:

4.

Date:
National Park:

5.

Date:
National Park:

6.

Date:
National Park:

7.

Date:
National Park:

8.

Date:
National Park:

9.

Date:
National Park:

10.

Date:
National Park:

COMPLETED ON:

BUCKET LIST:

1.

Date:
National Park:

2.

Date:
National Park:

3.

Date:
National Park:

4.

Date:
National Park:

5.

Date:
National Park:

6.

Date:
National Park:

7.

Date:
National Park:

8.

Date:
National Park:

9.

Date:
National Park:

10.

Date:
National Park:

COMPLETED ON:

BUCKET LIST:

1.

Date:
National Park:

2.

Date:
National Park:

3.

Date:
National Park:

4.

Date:
National Park:

5.

Date:
National Park:

6.

Date:
National Park:

7.

Date:
National Park:

8.

Date:
National Park:

9.

Date:
National Park:

10.

Date:
National Park:

COMPLETED ON:

ICONIC WILDLIFE SIGHTINGS

1. Alaskan Salmon
Date:
National Park:

2. American Alligator
Date:
National Park:

3. American Bison
Date:
National Park:

4. Bald Eagle
Date:
National Park:

5. Beaver
Date:
National Park:

6. Bighorn Sheep
Date:
National Park:

7. Black Bear
Date:
National Park:

8. Blue Whale
Date:
National Park:

9. Bobcat
Date:
National Park:

10. Brown Bear
Date:
National Park:

11. California Sea Lion
Date:
National Park:

12. Caribou
Date:
National Park:

13. Coyote
Date:
National Park:

14. Dall Sheep
Date:
National Park:

15. Dolphin
Date:

National Park:

16. Elk
Date:

National Park:

17. Fin Whale
Date:

National Park:

18. Fruit Bat
Date:

National Park:

19. Gila Monster
Date:

National Park:

20. Green Sea Turtle
Date:

National Park:

21. Grizzly Bear
Date:

National Park:

22. Harbor Seal
Date:

National Park:

23. Hawksbill Turtle
Date:

National Park:

24. Hummingbird
Date:

National Park:

25. Humpback Whale
Date:

National Park:

26. Jackrabbit
Date:

National Park:

27. Lynx
Date:

National Park:

28. Manatee
Date:

National Park:

29. Moose
Date:
National Park:

30. Mountain Goat
Date:
National Park:

31. Mule Deer
Date:
National Park:

32. Musk Ox
Date:
National Park:

33. Mustang
Date:
National Park:

34. Orca Whale
Date:
National Park:

35. Prairie Dog
Date:
National Park:

36. Puffin
Date:
National Park:

37. Rattlesnake
Date:
National Park:

38. Red Fox
Date:
National Park:

39. Sea Otter
Date:
National Park:

40. White-Tailed Deer
Date:
National Park:

41. Wolf
Date:
National Park:

42. Wolverine
Date:
National Park:

WHEN I VISITED:

WHO I WENT WITH:

WILDLIFE I SAW:

WHERE I STAYED:

FAVORITE EXPERIENCE:

WOULD I RETURN? yes/no

TOP 10 THINGS TO DO IN THIS PARK:

☆☆☆☆☆
☆☆☆☆☆
☆☆☆☆☆
☆☆☆☆☆
☆☆☆☆☆
☆☆☆☆☆
☆☆☆☆☆
☆☆☆☆☆
☆☆☆☆☆
☆☆☆☆☆

MY PARK RATINGS:

ACTIVITIES	FEW				MANY
SCENERY	DULL				SPECTACULAR
PEOPLE	CROWDED				PEACEFUL
WILDLIFE	NONE				LOTS
OVERALL	NOT FOR ME				LOVED IT!

• •

MOST MEMORABLE MOMENTS:

• •

SPACE TO JOURNAL / DRAW / COLLECT OFFICIAL NATIONAL PARK PASSPORT STAMPS:

WHEN I VISITED:

WHO I WENT WITH:

WILDLIFE I SAW:

WHERE I STAYED:

FAVORITE EXPERIENCE:

WOULD I RETURN? yes/no

TOP 10 THINGS TO DO IN THIS PARK:

☆☆☆☆☆
☆☆☆☆☆
☆☆☆☆☆
☆☆☆☆☆
☆☆☆☆☆
☆☆☆☆☆
☆☆☆☆☆
☆☆☆☆☆
☆☆☆☆☆
☆☆☆☆☆

MY PARK RATINGS:

ACTIVITIES	FEW				MANY
SCENERY	DULL				SPECTACULAR
PEOPLE	CROWDED				PEACEFUL
WILDLIFE	NONE				LOTS
OVERALL	NOT FOR ME				LOVED IT!

....

MOST MEMORABLE MOMENTS:

....

SPACE TO JOURNAL / DRAW / COLLECT OFFICIAL NATIONAL PARK PASSPORT STAMPS:

WHEN I VISITED:

WHO I WENT WITH:

WILDLIFE I SAW:

WHERE I STAYED:

FAVORITE EXPERIENCE:

WOULD I RETURN? yes/no

TOP 10 THINGS TO DO IN THIS PARK:

☆☆☆☆☆
☆☆☆☆☆
☆☆☆☆☆
☆☆☆☆☆
☆☆☆☆☆
☆☆☆☆☆
☆☆☆☆☆
☆☆☆☆☆
☆☆☆☆☆
☆☆☆☆☆

MY PARK RATINGS:

ACTIVITIES	FEW				MANY
SCENERY	DULL				SPECTACULAR
PEOPLE	CROWDED				PEACEFUL
WILDLIFE	NONE				LOTS
OVERALL	NOT FOR ME				LOVED IT!

· ·

MOST MEMORABLE MOMENTS:

· ·

SPACE TO JOURNAL / DRAW / COLLECT OFFICIAL NATIONAL PARK PASSPORT STAMPS:

WHEN I VISITED:

WHO I WENT WITH:

WILDLIFE I SAW:

WHERE I STAYED:

FAVORITE EXPERIENCE:

WOULD I RETURN? yes/no

TOP 10 THINGS TO DO IN THIS PARK:

☆ ☆ ☆ ☆ ☆
☆ ☆ ☆ ☆ ☆
☆ ☆ ☆ ☆ ☆
☆ ☆ ☆ ☆ ☆
☆ ☆ ☆ ☆ ☆
☆ ☆ ☆ ☆ ☆
☆ ☆ ☆ ☆ ☆
☆ ☆ ☆ ☆ ☆
☆ ☆ ☆ ☆ ☆
☆ ☆ ☆ ☆ ☆

MY PARK RATINGS:

ACTIVITIES	FEW				MANY
SCENERY	DULL				SPECTACULAR
PEOPLE	CROWDED				PEACEFUL
WILDLIFE	NONE				LOTS
OVERALL	NOT FOR ME				LOVED IT!

• •

MOST MEMORABLE MOMENTS:

• •

SPACE TO JOURNAL / DRAW / COLLECT OFFICIAL NATIONAL PARK PASSPORT STAMPS:

WHEN I VISITED:

WHO I WENT WITH:

WILDLIFE I SAW:

WHERE I STAYED:

FAVORITE EXPERIENCE:

WOULD I RETURN? yes/no

TOP 10 THINGS TO DO IN THIS PARK:

☆☆☆☆☆
☆☆☆☆☆
☆☆☆☆☆
☆☆☆☆☆
☆☆☆☆☆
☆☆☆☆☆
☆☆☆☆☆
☆☆☆☆☆
☆☆☆☆☆
☆☆☆☆☆

MY PARK RATINGS:

ACTIVITIES	FEW				MANY
SCENERY	DULL				SPECTACULAR
PEOPLE	CROWDED				PEACEFUL
WILDLIFE	NONE				LOTS
OVERALL	NOT FOR ME				LOVED IT!

• •

MOST MEMORABLE MOMENTS:

• •

SPACE TO JOURNAL / DRAW / COLLECT OFFICIAL
NATIONAL PARK PASSPORT STAMPS:

WHEN I VISITED:

WHO I WENT WITH:

WILDLIFE I SAW:

WHERE I STAYED:

FAVORITE EXPERIENCE:

WOULD I RETURN? yes/no

TOP 10 THINGS TO DO IN THIS PARK:

☆☆☆☆☆
☆☆☆☆☆
☆☆☆☆☆
☆☆☆☆☆
☆☆☆☆☆
☆☆☆☆☆
☆☆☆☆☆
☆☆☆☆☆
☆☆☆☆☆
☆☆☆☆☆

MY PARK RATINGS:

ACTIVITIES	FEW				MANY
SCENERY	DULL				SPECTACULAR
PEOPLE	CROWDED				PEACEFUL
WILDLIFE	NONE				LOTS
OVERALL	NOT FOR ME				LOVED IT!

....

MOST MEMORABLE MOMENTS:

....

SPACE TO JOURNAL / DRAW / COLLECT OFFICIAL NATIONAL PARK PASSPORT STAMPS:

WHEN I VISITED:

WHO I WENT WITH:

WILDLIFE I SAW:

WHERE I STAYED:

FAVORITE EXPERIENCE:

WOULD I RETURN? yes/no

TOP 10 THINGS TO DO IN THIS PARK:

☆☆☆☆☆
☆☆☆☆☆
☆☆☆☆☆
☆☆☆☆☆
☆☆☆☆☆
☆☆☆☆☆
☆☆☆☆☆
☆☆☆☆☆
☆☆☆☆☆
☆☆☆☆☆

MY PARK RATINGS:

ACTIVITIES	FEW				MANY
SCENERY	DULL				SPECTACULAR
PEOPLE	CROWDED				PEACEFUL
WILDLIFE	NONE				LOTS
OVERALL	NOT FOR ME				LOVED IT!

• •

MOST MEMORABLE MOMENTS:

• •

SPACE TO JOURNAL / DRAW / COLLECT OFFICIAL NATIONAL PARK PASSPORT STAMPS:

WHEN I VISITED:

WHO I WENT WITH:

WILDLIFE I SAW:

WHERE I STAYED:

FAVORITE EXPERIENCE:

WOULD I RETURN? yes/no

TOP 10 THINGS TO DO IN THIS PARK:

☆☆☆☆☆
☆☆☆☆☆
☆☆☆☆☆
☆☆☆☆☆
☆☆☆☆☆
☆☆☆☆☆
☆☆☆☆☆
☆☆☆☆☆
☆☆☆☆☆
☆☆☆☆☆

MY PARK RATINGS:

ACTIVITIES	FEW				MANY
SCENERY	DULL				SPECTACULAR
PEOPLE	CROWDED				PEACEFUL
WILDLIFE	NONE				LOTS
OVERALL	NOT FOR ME				LOVED IT!

....

MOST MEMORABLE MOMENTS:

....

SPACE TO JOURNAL / DRAW / COLLECT OFFICIAL NATIONAL PARK PASSPORT STAMPS:

WHEN I VISITED:

WHO I WENT WITH:

WILDLIFE I SAW:

WHERE I STAYED:

FAVORITE EXPERIENCE:

WOULD I RETURN? yes/no

TOP 10 THINGS TO DO IN THIS PARK:

☆☆☆☆☆
☆☆☆☆☆
☆☆☆☆☆
☆☆☆☆☆
☆☆☆☆☆
☆☆☆☆☆
☆☆☆☆☆
☆☆☆☆☆
☆☆☆☆☆
☆☆☆☆☆

MY PARK RATINGS:

ACTIVITIES	FEW				MANY
SCENERY	DULL				SPECTACULAR
PEOPLE	CROWDED				PEACEFUL
WILDLIFE	NONE				LOTS
OVERALL	NOT FOR ME				LOVED IT!

....

MOST MEMORABLE MOMENTS:

....

SPACE TO JOURNAL / DRAW / COLLECT OFFICIAL NATIONAL PARK PASSPORT STAMPS:

WHEN I VISITED:

WHO I WENT WITH:

WILDLIFE I SAW:

WHERE I STAYED:

FAVORITE EXPERIENCE:

WOULD I RETURN? yes/no

TOP 10 THINGS TO DO IN THIS PARK:

☆☆☆☆☆
☆☆☆☆☆
☆☆☆☆☆
☆☆☆☆☆
☆☆☆☆☆
☆☆☆☆☆
☆☆☆☆☆
☆☆☆☆☆
☆☆☆☆☆
☆☆☆☆☆

MY PARK RATINGS:

ACTIVITIES	FEW	MANY
SCENERY	DULL	SPECTACULAR
PEOPLE	CROWDED	PEACEFUL
WILDLIFE	NONE	LOTS
OVERALL	NOT FOR ME	LOVED IT!

· ·

MOST MEMORABLE MOMENTS:

· ·

SPACE TO JOURNAL / DRAW / COLLECT OFFICIAL NATIONAL PARK PASSPORT STAMPS:

GO EXPLORE

WANT A FREE NATIONAL PARKS GIFT?

Write an honest review of this national parks journal on Amazon and send a screenshot of your posted review to **hello@wildsimplicitypaper.com**. We'll reply with some national parks-related gifts you can print at home to plan and remember your adventures! *(Bonus points — and extra goodies! — if you include photos in your review.)*

Made in the USA
Las Vegas, NV
04 March 2024